MEGA
CREATIVITY
Five steps to thinking like a GENIUS

Andrei G. Aleinikov, Ph.D.

WALKING STICK PRESS
Cincinnati, Ohio
www.writersdigest.com

MegaCreativity: 5 Steps to Thinking Like a Genius. Copyright © 2002 by
Andrei G. Aleinikov. Manufactured in the United States of America. All rights
reserved. No part of this book may be reproduced in any form or by any
electronic or mechanical means including information storage and retrieval
systems without permission in writing from the publisher, except by a reviewer,
who may quote brief passages in a review. Published by Walking Stick Press,
an imprint of F&W Publications, Inc., 4700 East Galbraith Road, Cincinnati,
Ohio 45236. (800) 289-0963. First edition.

Visit our Web site at www.writersdigest.com for information on more resources
for writers.

To receive a free weekly e-mail newsletter delivering tips and updates about
writing and about Writer's Digest products, register directly at our Web site at
http://newsletters.fwpublications.com.

06   05   04   03   02   5   4   3   2   1

Library of Congress Cataloging-in-Publication Data

Aleinikov, Andrei G.
    Megacreativity : 5 steps to thinking like a genius / by Andrei G. Aleinikov.
        p.   cm.
    Includes index.
    ISBN 1-58297-150-1 (pbk.: alk. paper)   ISBN 1-58297-218-4 (hc.: alk. paper)
        1. Creative thinking. 2. Creative ability. I. Title.

    BF408 .A45 2002
    153.3'5—dc21   2002071373
                                                                          CIP

Edited by Jack Heffron and Meg Leder
Designed by Angela Wilcox
Cover by Melissa Riley/Tin Box Studio
Production coordinated by Sara Dumford

To my loving wife, Elena, and son, Andre.

To my family's new country, America! To Americans who gave us asylum in their hearts. To our new family: Jean and Pete Summer (our American Mom and Dad); Jeannette and Fran Hendryx; Pat and Stan Johns; Lola and Hartsell Northington; Liz and Pete Land; Janice and Rabbi David Baylinson; Cameron and John Napier; Marge Payne; Thomas Hinds; Helen, Irving, and Jeffrey Bern; Louisa and Michael Weinrib; Philip and Michelle Goodwin; Susan and Michael Newman; Harry and Jeanne Wilkins; Clare Weil; Eileen Heninger; David Chalkley; and our dearest American friends who saved our lives, helped us, cared about us, and gave us an opportunity to make this quantum leap to the future.

acknowledgments

If this book is worth anything, then it is only because I am standing on the shoulders of the giants—my teachers. This leap to new methodologies that work so fast and effectively both in the business and educational environments could not have happened without my great teachers in creativity.

I am in awe of Dr. E. Paul Torrance, the "Creativity Man." It was his trust that made me the editor of the book *The Future of Creativity*, which combines the efforts of top creativity minds to look into the future.

Special thanks to Dr. Sidney J. Parnes, whose work I was translating for a publication in the five-volume edition of *Creative Management*, Russian Academy of Sciences. Sid and Bea Parnes's help and hospitality enriched my life.

We love and cherish our friends, but we need their courage and patience to get things done. Dr. Kobus Neethling, a "beyonder" who makes South Africa a leader in the creativity movement, is one of those friends who will help you climb the vertical cliff on the way to the peak. Kobus was instrumental in helping me attempt the Guinness world record for the fastest written and fastest published book (*Making the Impossible Possible: 200 Plus Creative Ideas*, 2001). Another peak climber, Lisa Spragens, also assisted in this attempt through her work with preliminary accelerated publications, including *Loving Creativity*, 2000.

I also am grateful to the following courageous and visionary principals and directors who dared to believe in a new approach: Larry Black (The Greening Center, Kansas City, Missouri), John Magee (Franklin Junior High School, Franklin, Ohio), Jenny Law (Singapore), and many others.

They made it possible for their students to experience the new pedagogy as a "breath of fresh air."

I treasure the recollections of my first teachers in creativity, Alexander Romanov and Victor Sigalov, whose humor, knowledge, and dedication made me addicted to creativity. I also extend my highest appreciation to my scientific mentor, Dr. Maryam S. Karayeva—a role model and the finest thinker I've ever met. Oh, how I miss her!

Heartfelt thanks to my many American friends who helped my family and I discover and appreciate a new life in America and to the Jewish community who gave us loving support and a new feeling of identity.

Lots of thanks are due to my editor, Jack Heffron, who "found" me at the University of Cincinnati where I was creating a workshop for professors and children. I deeply appreciate his vision and dedication.

Finally, this book would not have been written without the constant support and even sacrifice of my family: my wife, Elena, the co-author of several articles, the patient partner in developing new ideas, and the inspiration for nearly everything I have done; and my son, Andrei (artistic name Andre Kohn), the co-author of my inventions, who at the age of eleven became the youngest inventor in the Soviet Union and who now is the best example of creativity principles at work—a well-known artist in Scottsdale, Arizona.

Last, but not least, to my readers, my students, and my friends—you are the eternal inspiration! It is your inquisitive eyes that I look into while I write. It is in your minds and hearts that I hope to kindle the spark during my seminars and workshops. Thank you for inspiring me!

 People say one has to have guts to do what Dr. Andy Aleinikov is doing. An American citizen since May 2002, Dr. Aleinikov was a Russian colonel only ten years ago when he was selected to be the first Russian student at the U.S. Air Force Air War College. When he decided to remain in the United States, he sacrificed his career, his honors, and his ranks to give his family religious and spiritual freedom. Moreover, by risking his life when defecting, he saved his scientific discoveries for humanity: new sciences, MegaCreativity, and superpowerful methodologies of human development that otherwise could have been misused or hidden in the dungeons of military secrets.

Dr. Aleinikov (a.k.a. "Dr. Andy," "Mega-Creator," and "Crazy Russian") is a world-renowned keynote speaker, scientific pioneer, consultant, and educational leader who has changed the lives of thousands of people around the world. He is the 2001 Dr. E. Paul Torrance Lecturer at the University of Georgia.

Dr. Aleinikov is "the world's leading expert on Mega-Creativity" and the founder of two new sciences, including *Novology*, the science of newness. He is the author and editor of over one hundred books and articles on innovation, creativity, and language, including his book *Mega-Creator: From Creativity to Mega-, Giga-, and Infi-Creativity* (1999). His articles are featured in *Encyclopedia of Creativity* (1999) and *World Education Encyclopedia* (2002). He is the editor of *The Future of Creativity* (2002), a monograph published by the Dr. E. Paul Torrance Annual Lecture Series.

His business clients are colleges, universities, and small and big companies, including such innovative Fortune 500 companies as 3M Company, Procter and Gamble, and Southern Company. His projects are unique. He unites famous researchers and children in the book *Creating Creativity: 101 Definitions (What Webster Never Told You)* (2000), and he makes the entire student body (over four hundred children) of Franklin Junior High School (Franklin, Ohio) "instant authors" of the book *And the World Would Be a Better Place* (2000).

Dr. Aleinikov teaches Psychology of Creativity, Linguistics, Communication, Creative and Innovative Education, and Creativity and Innovation in Business at Troy State University Montgomery, Alabama, where he became a recipient of the President's Excellence Award in 1999. He also is the founding president of the Mega-Innovative Mind International Institute and the School of Geniuses, which implement his unique educational system *Genius*. This system, which discovers a genius in every child, is now being implemented in Singapore. He is the founding president of the Alabama chapter of the American Creativity Association and the president of the Montgomery chapter of Phi Delta Kappa (PDK, Association of International Educators).

His wife, Elena (maiden name Kohn), is the executive director of the F. Scott and Zelda Fitzgerald Museum in Montgomery, and she plays violin with the Montgomery Symphony Orchestra. They have a son, Andre Kohn, who is a well-known artist living in Scottsdale, Arizona.

table of contents

Step
One *Quit Quitting!*

Step
Two *Why Not Every (K)not?*

Step
Three *Go for a Million*

The question is, who is interested in creativity? And
my answer is that practically everybody is. This
interest is no longer confined to psychologists and
psychiatrists. Now it has become a question of
national and international policy as well.

ABRAHAM MASLOW

You've probably picked up this book and decided to read
a bit of it, the introduction anyway, to find out what this
guy, Andy Aleinikov, means by MegaCreativity. These actions show me that you are a creative person, engaged by
the world around you, anxious to make some larger contri-
bution to that world by being a more creative person.

The next choice you have to make is whether to read
the book and master the techniques that will launch you to
MegaCreativity. It is your choice. You can choose to live a
more creative life. You can choose to be creative in small
steps (smaller achievements) or creative in large steps (bigger achievements). In mathematical terms, you can choose
DecaCreativity ($\times$ 10), HectoCreativity ($\times$ 100), KiloCrea-
tivity ($\times$ 1000), or even MegaCreativity ($\times$ 1,000,000). It's
up to you. If creators and innovators are winners and
achievers, then MegaCreators and MegaInnovators are . . .

WARNING

Do not read this book if you are a misoneist (a person
who hates newness).

Do not read this book if you are a reactionary, a retro-
grade, a regressive bureaucrat.

Do not read this book if you are a coward or an "ostrich."
Do not read this book if you like monotonous routines.
Do not read this book if you are against daydreaming.
This book is for those who:

- love fun (new things, humor, mind flexibility).
- love to look into the future.
- love bold ideas and courageous actions.
- love to make a difference.
- love to daydream.

This book is for those who dare to dream and dare to act, those who revolve the Earth, those who are shakers and makers. MegaCreativity offers you a new way of thinking as well as methods for expanding your mind, giving you the power to create more powerful and more plentiful ideas. The process is easy and difficult at the same time. (Who told you that becoming a genius could be easy?) However, the system works—it has been tested on audiences all over the world, and these people have learned to expand their creativity.

Let's get started with the following quiz.

INSANITY/SANITY QUIZ

Question 1

Year: 1800. The world is in chaos. Epidemics of plague, measles, typhoid fever, malaria, and cholera kill millions of people.

You are sitting at a table eating lunch when a physician comes to you and says he has developed a way to prevent disease rather than treating it later and losing millions of people. He also has a dream that someday, deadly diseases like plagues will be eradicated. His name, Edward Jenner, tells you nothing. After you hear about his dream, what do you do?

    A. Smile, consider him crazy, and send him away.

    B. Order the servants to kick him out.

    C. Get interested and involved.

    D. Nod, yawn, and forget about it.

Question 2

Year: 1900. Horses are the basic means of transportation, but bikes and cars are becoming fashionable. There are no traffic rules yet, so every day people are killed in the streets. Officials consider limiting the speed limit to three miles per hour on the turns and twelve miles per hour on the streets. Also, a year ago the government declared that all inventions had been made—nothing new could be invented—so the U.S. Patent and Trademark Office was closed.

You are sitting at a table eating lunch when two mechanics come to you and say they can build a flying machine. They also have a dream that in the future all people will be able to fly in these machines. They say they are the Wright brothers, but their name means nothing to you. After you hear their story, what do you do?

    A. Smile, consider them crazy, and send them away.

    B. Order the servants to kick them out.

    C. Get interested and involved.

    D. Nod, yawn, and forget about it.

Question 3

Year: 2000. Many deadly diseases have been eradicated. Planes are everywhere. Still, the world's school systems suffer from violence, drug problems, and high rates of teen pregnancy. Students score low on tests, have little discipline, and show no respect to adults.

You are sitting at a table having lunch when a guy comes to you and says he has found a way to prevent all educational diseases. He also has a dream that in ten to fifteen years schools will be different: Students will want to go to school, and teachers will punish the least diligent students by saying, "You've worked lower than your potential today, so tomorrow you will stay at home. We will do our class adventures without you." When you hear this dream, what do you do?

A. Smile, consider him crazy, and send him away.

B. Order the waiters to kick him out.

C. Get interested and involved.

D. Nod, yawn, and forget about it.

If your answer was anything but C for any of these questions, it's time to open up to newness, innovation, and possibility. Dreamers make this world dramatically better. Have a dream! Given that you have read this far, I am convinced that you are a creative thinker, someone who is engaged by the world and who is anxious to learn ways to be more creative—to be a MegaCreator. If I'm right, please read on.

You've probably realized that the guy in the third question is me. I have a dream of improving our educational system and the methods we use for learning. You'll find these methods in this book. Let's dream and work together to change the world.

ANDY ALEINIKOV, PH.D.

Quit Quitting!

Genius is a strategic advantage (like Einstein).

Genius is the savior (like Archimedes).

Genius is the future (like Edison).

Genius is the glory for the country (like Alexander
of Macedonia—Alexander the Great).

Genius is the resource bigger than oil and gas
resources because genius can discover that gas and
oil are not needed (like Roentgen).

Genius is forever (like Socrates) . . .

ALEANDR

Achieving the level of genius will take some action on your
part. You will be asked to *do* things. Becoming a genius
is not just knowing that it is possible—it is taking action
and having genius experiences. The first section of this
book deals with the First Law of MegaCreativity: Quit
Quitting. So get ready for action. Are you ready? I ask my
audiences to answer aloud, and I want you to do it, too.

If your voice is soft and unsure, make it loud and confident. This book needs your commitment.

I will ask you again, "Are you ready?"

If your answer is a loud and confident "Yes," please
turn the page.

Chapter One

Open Your Mind

Towards the door we never opened.

T.S. ELIOT

Let's start. Find a stopwatch or put your wristwatch in front of you. Get a pen or a pencil and a piece of paper if you don't want to write in the book. As the author, however, I would be happy to see this book scribbled through and dog-eared. It would mean that you read it, you thought about it, you acted upon it, and your mind was awake.

PERSPECTIVE PROBLEMS

Let's start with some funny problems just to check your perspectives. They were invented so long ago that I don't know who originally created them. I suspect that the second problem was mentioned in one of the popular books by Russian author Vladimir Levi.

Note: I meaningfully used the word *problem*, not *test*, because I am not testing you, and you are not testing yourself. You are checking your own tendencies to find out where and how you can move further.

Problem 1

You have only five seconds for this exercise.

Take a pen or a pencil and draw a very big circle on a separate sheet of paper like the circle below. Put a dot somewhere on the sheet of paper.

The answer to this problem is coming later, so proceed with the next exercise.

Problem 2

This must be done as fast as possible.

Write down an odd number up to ten: _____

Again, the answer to this problem is coming later. Here's another exercise for you.

Problem 3

Whether my class is a group of children in the School of Geniuses or a group of adults at a company like 3M Company, Procter and Gamble, or Southern Company, we usually begin with some warm-up exercises. Here is a popular one.

Write down a three-digit number. Next, find the word in the first column in the table below that corresponds to the first digit you wrote. Then do the same for your second and third digits, using the second and third columns.

Simple words	Complicated words (for fun)	What I like to add
1. dog	1. tetrahedron	1. anticipation
2. cat	2. euthanasia	2. blueness
3. house	3. quark	3. constitution
4. book	4. metabolism	4. confrontation
5. snow	5. synchronizer	5. constipation
6. room	6. ventriloquist	6. excavation
7. light	7. escapist	7. exhumation
8. lamp	8. etymology	8. exclusivity
9. chair	9. cosmetology	9. dullness

For example, if your three-digit number was 232, then your combination would look like this: cat (first row), quark (second row), and blueness (third row).

When you have three words, write five sentences and use all three words in each sentence. You have only five minutes for this task.

TURN THE PAGE

FOR THE

NEXT STEP

Note: If you jumped to this page without finishing all three exercises, you are impatient, you dislike discipline, you hate long tasks, and you prefer instant gratification. In a normal school, you would be punished for this, but in an unusual school like ours—the school of creativity, the school of life—you are okay. You are certainly creative! However, to check *how* creative you are, it is better for you to go through the exercises in the order they are given. Do you think patience and workability are important for a genius? Thomas Edison was impatient, but only with impatient people. If you're impatient but you persevere, compare yourself to him.

If you are truly through with the sentences, go to the next section.

ANSWERS

Problem 1

Check where you put your dot on the sheet:

- Disciplined and well-schooled people have a tendency to stay within the lines, so they put the dot in the center of the circle.
- More carefree people tend to put the dot anywhere in the circle but the center. The closer the dot is to the edge, the riskier the person.
- Seldom, but occasionally, people put the dot on the line. Interesting . . . as if there is no other space on the sheet! These people may be law enforcement officers or lawyers (rule makers).
- Some people who are either careless or brave put the dot outside of the circle (anywhere on the page).

- Very few people turn the page and make a dot on the other side. That may be a sign of a genius.

Problem 2

Here is the task with your odd numbers:

- If you chose 9, you are an adventurer (and you probably put your dot as close to the line as possible in the previous problem).
- If you wrote 7, you are normal.
- If you wrote 5, you are talented.
- If you wrote 3, you may be in love with fairy tales, stories, and history.
- If you wrote 1, you are a genius. (Ha-ha! It's that simple!)

The problem certainly looks like a joke, but there is some truth in every joke. A genius would probably choose the answer that is as far as possible from the task ("up to ten") yet that's still the simplest odd number (1). An adventurer would prefer the number closest to the named limit (9). A talented person would choose safe but winning middle ground (5). Most people choose 7, which is why it's considered normal. That's also why so many best-selling books use "Seven Steps" or "Seven Habits"—publishers know the number appeals to a large number of people. Finally, people who choose 3 are far enough from "up to ten" to be resistant to the task (the present). They prefer a safer solution—the past or history.

This explanation may seem unscientific, and I caution you not to put too much weight in the outcome, but still there is some validity. We can certainly predict that the number of individuals who choose *7* will be significantly higher than the number of individuals who choose *1*. Want to test it? Try it on your friends. Does it seem to correlate with what you know about them?

Problem 3

First, how many sentences did you write? Three? Four? My question is not to those who wrote two, three, or four sentences. You probably ran out of time, right? My question is to those who wrote five and had time to write more. Why didn't you write six? Or seven?

A typical answer to this question is: "You said to make five, and I made five. Why should I make more?"

When I hear such an answer, I say, "Right! Blame it on the professor!"

Here is the reality.

In traditional schools, we are given tasks, we are taught to follow them, and we are conditioned to conform to the rules of the task. When students fail to solve a problem, the first thing they do is take the "blame it on the professor" position: "You didn't show us how to do it!" Another attitude that many people take is: "Somebody is to blame—not me. If I failed the exam, the teacher is to blame: She didn't teach me properly. If there's a conflict in my family, family members are to blame: They didn't come to me to talk about it. If the interview went wrong, the interviewers are to blame: He asked stupid questions."

If you find yourself saying such things, then you have put other people in charge of your life. You are the puppet, and you let other people pull the strings. It seems that people can do whatever they want with you. This attitude also causes many problems in the world—at school, at home, at work. We blame other people instead of being responsible and taking action.

A much more powerful position is to be in charge of yourself. When you fail, as we all do, take responsibility. Instead of feeling like a victim, you will feel powerful and in control. You will hear a new, much stronger voice:

"I failed the exam. It is my fault—I will study the material again."

"There is a conflict in my family. It is my fault. I was not communicating properly—let me learn more about communication."

"I botched the interview. It is my fault—let me study interview techniques."

As a result, you become more knowledgeable; next time, you win. Being knowledgeable is a powerful position, one that will lead you to new heights of creativity and success. Some people might say there is danger in such a position. Everything seems to be your fault, and soon you are crying in the corner or feeling frustrated. The word *everything* leads you into this trap. Things never come together—they come one after the other. We address one wrongdoing after another, and if we are quick enough in taking measures to change the situation, we face the challenge, change our behavior, and win. With this approach, we grow. If we don't take responsibility and don't try to change, things accumulate, thus becoming "everything."

Avoid being passive. Be active in the face of adversity, or adversity will continue.

It is your choice to make. Make it now!

❑ "I am weak. I want to stay weak. Others are in charge of my life."

❑ "I am strong. I want to be stronger. I am in charge of my life."

If you prefer the second option, then we can go further.

Please recall your schooling again. In class you studied, for instance, chapter sixteen, and for your homework assignment your teacher gave you problems 1, 3, and 5 to solve. When you came home, did you also solve problems 2, 4, and 6? No!

Why? Did you think if you solved them, your brain would be damaged permanently?

Here comes the typical answer: "Why should I solve them?"

Okay. Any of you go to the gym? Why? To train your muscles? What do you do to train your muscles? Do you lift a feather in your hands, or do you lift weights? Why do you lift weights? Because you want some tension to challenge your muscles! Tension makes muscles grow. They will not be tense if you use a feather.

Your brain is your "thinking muscle." It must be trained. Do you prefer it to stay inflexible and lazy? Do you prefer the feather to the real weights? There is nothing bad in feeling that way. I felt it. I was in school, too. And I remember the feelings. The tendency was to do as little as possible, as quickly as possible, so you could have fun doing another activity. Right?

Understandable, but strategically wrong. In school we

did not work the main muscle—the one that controls all other muscles, controls all our activities, and ultimately all our lives. The brain is this muscle—the "success muscle." You can't use any other muscle if you do not have the brain.

So it is time for your decision again. Check it:

❑ "I am *not* going to train my brain because I want to be stupid."

❑ "I am going to train my brain because it is my means of achieving success."

If you prefer the first option, put the book aside. If you prefer the second option, then I can give you the first secret to becoming a genius. There is one big difference between normal (or normalized) people and creative people: Creative people never stop. They begin to do something, they become involved, and they do not want to stop.

So, the First Law of MegaCreativity is Quit Quitting.

Say it aloud: Quit Quitting!

What do you think it means?

Yes, never stop. Yes, never quit. Yes, keep on keeping on.

Quit Quitting is paradoxical: If we quit quitting, do we still quit?

Because it is paradoxical, people remember it. Say it several times with different intonations. Follow this law. Quit Quitting is the cornerstone of MegaCreativity. The next time I ask you to write five sentences, how many will you do? If you say, "Six, seven, nine, as many as I can," then you are on the way to genius thinking. However, the number of sentences is only one aspect—the quantitative aspect. We also have to consider the other aspect—qualitative. How good are your sentences? Are they funny? Are they impressive? Original? Before we delve into the issue of quality, we'll first examine some myths about the nature of genius—myths that could hold you back from reaching your true creative potential. So as T.S. Eliot says, let's step "towards the door we never opened."

Chapter Two

Understand the Nature of Genius

When Nature has work to be done, she creates a
genius to do it.

RALPH WALDO EMERSON

The nature of genius is traditionally surrounded by a number of misleading myths. Maybe people are intimidated or even frightened by the concept of genius. Whatever the reason, these myths need to be debunked.

MYTH 1: "GENIUSES ARE BORN."

This idea is quite common but incorrect. Why? Genetics does influence our lives, but it does not determine them completely. If this were true, why wouldn't we lock up the children of mass murderers at birth? Why wouldn't we forego school for those who were predisposed to squander it? The world would probably be much more efficient and less chaotic—and less interesting—if people were that easy to classify. Upbringing, the social influence, is as important as genetic heritage. Even with the best genetic material possible, without a positive social influence and learned skills, a person can't achieve genius.

An analogy may show it more vividly. Marble is a beautiful but raw material. It is the hard labor of the sculptor that transforms the marble from a piece of rock into a world-class museum piece. On the other hand, a clumsy sculptor may shatter the marble into pieces, and the result will end up in a trash can. The potential in every person is like a piece of marble—and whether each person will end up in jail or in the Hall of Fame depends upon his or her learned skills.

Secondly, the phrase "Geniuses are born" is used as an excuse for laziness—a reason to not work hard. In reality, we are all born weak and needy. A baby will die if left without care for a week. On the other hand, a baby will smile happily and grow quickly when properly taken care of. Geniuses are made by loving people: mothers, fathers, grandparents, and other adults who spend their lives sharing their goals, wisdom, and love with the future lights of the world.

MYTH 2: "GENIUSES ARE RECOGNIZED IN CHILDHOOD."

This myth comes from confusing the notions of *prodigy* and *genius*. It implies that if a child is not recognized as a genius in childhood, then he or she is not a genius. Actually, it is prodigies who are recognized in childhood; a prodigy is an individual who shows adult-level results in childhood. Genius is different. Albert Einstein, for example, who could not speak until the age of three, was a dyslexic who had countless difficulties in school. Pablo Picasso managed to get through school only with his father sitting nearby during classes. Thomas Edison got Cs in physics. Robert Frost published his first book at the age of thirty-eight. Peter Roget created his famous thesaurus after retirement at the age of seventy. Michailo Lomonosov (the founder of Moscow University) was considered illiterate because he couldn't read Greek and Latin. At the age of nineteen, when he came from a far northern village to Moscow "to study," he had to attend elementary school.

Could anyone at Edison's or Einstein's school predict that the two men were future geniuses? Did any of the seven-year-old kids who were laughing and mocking nineteen-year-old Lomonosov, or the teachers giving him a wry grin, ever think that they were degrading the future founder of modern Russian science, the "one-man university"? No.

Taking all this into consideration, would anyone dare to predict today that this or that particular child or adult will *not* be a genius in the coming years? The philosophy of the School of Geniuses is very different. We know and openly state that there is a genius within every child and person. Therefore, let us consciously alter the statement, "Geniuses are recognized in childhood" and promote a new statement: "Let us recognize a genius in every child and person."

MYTH 3: "GENIUSES ARE SUPERIOR PEOPLE WHO ARE TALENTED IN EVERYTHING."

Yes, there are geniuses like Leonardo da Vinci, Johann Wolfgang von Goethe, and Lomonosov who are immortalized both in science and in the arts. But there are so many others—Ludwig van Beethoven, who was deaf, and Helen Keller, who was blind—who show conclusively that even those who are seemingly beyond the margin *can* be geniuses, let alone normally developed or even gifted children. With the proof so simple, I truly believe, and my research corroborates it, that every child and person can be a genius. History shows that every child and person has a chance.

What did all of these geniuses have in common? Strong character and somebody loving them and believing in them. The fathers of Wolfgang Mozart and Niccolò Paganini made their sons geniuses. Psychological literature is filled with factual stories such as theirs. If you weren't so lucky as a child, you still have a chance. Do you have someone who loves you and believes in you now? Use the power they give to you. If you have no one, you must love yourself and believe in yourself.

MYTH 4: "GENIUSES ARE CRAZY."

Before we analyze this phrase, let's take a little less offensive point of view: A genius and an insane person are two points of a cut-and-opened circle. Cut a circle in any place, put your fingers on both sides of the cut, and open the circle. The two points that were so close to each other now go in different directions and stay as far apart as possible.

Another way I understand the concept of "craziness," or "sickness," is due to my father-in-law, Dr. Nickolai N. Kon, a Russian psychiatrist who was the founder of psychiatric service in Volgograd (Stalingrad). He said that there are sick people who are normal, and there are healthy people who are abnormal. Under "normal" in this case, he meant that if a person is sick (mentally), but is interested in life, cares for the others, and produces positive results, then this person is normal. On the other hand, if a person is healthy (mentally), but behaves like a destroyer, acting only in his own interests, then this person is abnormal.

This is an interesting idea. A person like Vincent Van Gogh may be sick but considered normal because he was producing innovative and positive results. A person like Adolf Hitler might be healthy (which I personally doubt), but considered abnormal because he was catastrophically destructive.

I can also add that often it is not the genius who is crazy, but the society. Consider the biblical story of King Herod. He gave an order to massacre all the male newborn babies in the hopes of killing the one would-be future king. Wasn't that crazy? Consider other examples. Geordano Bruno was burnt by the Inquisition for his belief in the existence of many worlds like ours. What's wrong with that? Galileo was tortured and pressed to officially reject his "heretic" views in order to stay alive—and his views were about the Earth revolving. Tomaso Campanella secretly wrote his utopia (*City of the Sun*) on scraps of paper while jailed for many years; he dared to think about a future society where all people were equal. Socrates was tried, sentenced, and executed just for his talks with young people at the market. These are the ways that past (and often insane) societies fight against the future. Albert Einstein, as a more contemporary example, was lucky enough to exist in a more civilized society; otherwise, he could have suffered the same fate.

So, roughly speaking, geniuses have the same chance of ending up in the mad house as the rest of the world. However, there is one large *but*: Geniuses will be remembered. Those who are not geniuses and who end up in mental hospitals will merely be medical statistics.

MYTH 5: "GENIUS IS ACCIDENTAL."

This point of view comes from *serendipity*, the science of accidental discoveries. Wilhelm Roentgen, for example, discovered radioactivity when he inadvertently left some materials on film packed in black paper. He accidentally developed it and found strange white spots on the developed film. That meant some unknown rays (X rays) were penetrating the black paper that was usually impenetrable by normal rays. One could say Roentgen was lucky, but others don't necessarily consider this a serendipitous accident. Consider the following: How often does a normal person work with radioactive materials and have film nearby to even make such a mistake? Roentgen was a researcher. He was coming to that discovery; a day earlier, or a day later—it had to happen. Moreover, at that time research was going on in many laboratories; if not Roentgen, then somebody else would have made the same more or less "accidental" discovery. Finally, the others—less ready for the discovery or not intelligent enough to see it as one—would say that the film was bad and would never connect the white spots on it to the strange penetrating rays. Geniuses are profound searchers. They stay on the cutting edge all the time, which is why they always seem to be there at the "right" time.

As you can see, many myths surround the idea of genius. To achieve MegaCreativity, ignore them. Such wrong-headed beliefs keep us from achieving our full potentials. They allow us to be lazy; they tell us that people will think we are crazy if we offer challenging new ideas; they tell us we will be outcasts; they tell us it is too late to achieve our creative potentials. All wrong! Nature has so much work to be done that she creates us all to do it. Nature creates individual or group geniuses to do the job. As the honorable judge, Vanzetta P. McPherson, said during my naturalization ceremony, "The genius of America is not that it is what it ought to be; the genius of America is that it continues to try to be what it can be." So whether it is a person, a group of individuals, or a country, a genius, in my opinion, is a *super recognized super innovator*. In simple terms, a genius is very broadly recognized (over borders and over centuries) for his or her enormously innovative deeds that benefited society. Now that you are free from the mythology surrounding genius, let's move on and discover the genius in you.

Chapter Three

Discover the Genius in Your Inner Child

> My genius is no more than a girl.
>
> If she with ivory
>
> fingers drives a tune through the lyre,
>
> we look at the process.

EZRA POUND

When I speak about genius, I usually say that there is a potential genius in every child. Therefore, the task of a parent or educator is to develop this potential to the fullest, that is, the genius level.

I say "in every child" because (1) I have not seen children incapable of learning (if they are mentally healthy), (2) there is no logical foundation for excluding any child from the list of potential geniuses, and (3) there is a child within all of us.

No one can predict the future. As Clayton M. Christensen, the author of *The Innovator's Dilemma*, states while writing about disruptive technologies, "always count on one anchor: *Experts' opinions will always be wrong.*"

Certainly, two hundred years ago no one could have imagined that we would have cars, airplanes, spaceships, or television. Forty years ago no one could have predicted that computers would be in almost every American home. Even visionary people fail in their attempts to predict the future. Bill Gates was quoted as saying, "Sixty-four kilobytes [of memory] ought to be plenty for anyone." Of course, now we are using sixty-four megabytes of memory (a thousand times as much), and it is still not enough for many people. No one could have imagined or predicted that the skills of fast typing on a keyboard and fast reading from a computer screen would be valuable. No one could have foreseen that handling the controls in an aircraft and being able to do it for a long time would make such legends (flying geniuses?) as Charles Lindbergh.

Even a child who is weakly developed in some areas could turn out to be needed by future societies and could save millions of people (for example, Edward Jenner, the inventor of the vaccination). A particular individual also can become the discoverer of a whole new field or the first specialist in a field. How can we—adults, teachers, or parents—know this field, which does not exist yet? If we cannot, then what right do we have to judge who will or will not become a genius?

That's why I say, "Every child is a potential genius." There is no way to know which particular features the future will require, so I treat every child in the classroom like he or she is a future genius. Life will show where a child's potential will lead and where his or her potential will blossom and be realized.

When I teach a course to adults, I often hear, "So it is not too late? Even for me?"

The answer is, "It is never too late."

Just like Peter M. Roget published his thesaurus at the

age of seventy-three after retiring from a career in medicine. Just like Vincent Van Gogh and Paul Gauguin took
their first arts classes in their late thirties. There is no
such a thing as being too late. The question is: What field
is good for you? Where are your interests? Where is your
passion? Is there undiscovered terrain that needs to be
explored? Is there something you could make that is so
revolutionary it will surprise your contemporaries and
turn out to be invaluably useful for the future?

When people say to me, "It's not too late?" I see hope
in their eyes.

There is a child living in every one of us. This child
likes to play. He thinks of unusual things and is a dreamer.
He may grow older, but he never becomes old. This child
shows up in the twinkle of the eye, the burst of laughter,
the cunning smile, the risky joke, and the adventurous
mood. Sometimes this child is unwelcome in our normalized reality. He is called a rebel, a hooligan, a jerk. He may
be a quiet but inquisitive observer.

As adults we might be normalized, beaten, and
straightened out; however, the child inside each of us remains unchanged. She calls to the stars, drives people
nuts, howls at the moon, and does many other seemingly
foolish things. Beyond the restraints of time and space,
this inner child has unending curiosity, unlimited energy,
and enormous goals.

Our bodies become older, our faces wrinkle, our or-
gans become sick, our souls become tired, but our spirits
are alive. It is this spirit—this inner child—that makes us
younger. And this child is a genius—or is ready to be one,
or is in the process of becoming one!

Start here. List the five "most stupid" things you would dream of doing.

1. _____

2. _____

3. _____

4. _____

5. _____

_____

_____

_____

_____

CHECK YOURSELF

In step one, you decided to Quit Quitting. You promised to give six, seven, eight answers, or as many as you could, when you are asked to give five. Did you keep your promise with this exercise?

I structured your writing space intentionally. I left additional space for you, and I left some space for other answers. Have you followed the law of Quit Quitting? Did you fill the sixth line? The seventh? Have you made an effort to do more than you have been asked to do?

I hope you did. I also hope you now understand that the mystery of a genius is not so mysterious. A genius pushes beyond requirements and expectations. If you broke the First Law, avoid berating yourself. It takes time to begin thinking like a genius. But do go back to the exercise, and this time, follow the first law. It is unreasonable to think you'll become outstanding if you only do what other people do—normal things, things that are usual, traditional, trivial. If you learned to make more than you were asked and if in all my previous tasks you were making more than five, then you have made the first big step to becoming a genius. Congratulations!

Just remember, your genius is like a child. This genius does something (like we did our exercise) and also watches the process, as Ezra Pound says. A genius has an ability to see two levels where other people see only one. Now you can do it: You write something, and you think of writing more. Welcome to the genius world!

Why Not Every (K)not?

If at first the idea is not absurd, then there is no hope
for it.

ALBERT EINSTEIN

In this section I will explain creativity as the main feature
of genius, I will prove that we are all creative, and I will
show you how to increase your creativity to where it will
be more powerful than that of a natural genius. You can
do this only by using special methods of boosting creativity that will give you the strength and skills to surpass
even the most talented and gifted individuals. In other
words, in this step you will open your mind to incredible
opportunities—to MegaCreativity and even AbsoluteCreativity. For many, MegaCreativity may seem like an absurd idea. So, according to Einstein, there *is* hope for it.

Chapter Four

Say "Yes" to Possibility and Impossibility

Probable impossibilities are to be preferred to improbable possibilities.

ARISTOTLE

I asked Sid Parnes, the founder of the Creative Problem Solving movement and the Creative Education Foundation, what he thought was the most important prerequisite for creativity. He replied with one word: "openness."

If the first section of this book taught you to continue working and trying, to push beyond expectations, then it actually taught you to *open up* to new quantitative horizons—to try more than you usually do. Truly, there is much more to gain if you continue to work longer on something.

It is like physical movement: Imagine yourself standing in the middle of your house. If you move two, three, five, seven, or even ten steps in one direction, how much newness do you see? It is still the same house or the same yard that you know. Now imagine moving one hundred, five hundred, or seven hundred steps away from your house. Do you see more that is new? Imagine moving one hundred, one thousand, or twenty thousand miles away from your house. Has your perspective changed? Do you see many new sights? Discoveries—new things to see and experience—are all around you. You must be ready to take these extra steps, because the farther you travel, the higher the probability that you will make a discovery. Be ready to make these large-scale steps. Use the ideas we discussed in the first step—quit quitting, free yourself from the mythology surrounding genius, and work with your inner child.

However, producing more of something is not enough. You can work many hours and still not move through all the trivial solutions to find more creative ones. Also, if you do the same things over and over again (or in the same manner), you achieve the same results. Being open and trying different things is the first step, but now we must find ways to accelerate this process and get to the original, or higher quality ideas, faster. To open up to new and better qualitative horizons, we have to master other methods.

To feel like a creator (and because it's fun), scribble your definition of creativity on this page. Avoid looking at dictionaries or other sourcebooks. Just write your own definition in your own terms. You can jot the first thing that comes to mind, or you can mull it over. Either way, go ahead and write it before you continue reading.

_____

_____

_____

_____

_____

_____

_____

_____

_____

Did you write a definition?

If not, then you have broken the First Law. Back up and jot something down. If you wrote a definition, good for you. You have taken the first step.

TAKING THE FIRST STEP

As an educator and a presenter, I know that some people are shy and find it difficult to take the first step. There are two objections I hear often: (1) "I don't know anything about creativity" and (2) "I'm afraid to look stupid because my definition is not perfect."

Please note that both the first and the second statements contain _not_ and both of them mean "no": "I do _not_ know anything . . . and that is why I give _no_ definition"; "My definition is _not_ perfect . . . and that is why I give _no_ definition."

I understand your difficulties, and it means that we need an exercise to push past that "no."

Let's slow down and try a smaller task.

Here are three adjectives: _round, sour, yellow._

Please list objects that would fit these three adjectives. When I say "fit," I mean that the object you are talking about would be round, sour, and yellow—apply all three adjectives to one object.

You have three minutes for this. Okay, go!

_____

_____

_____

_____

_____

_____

_____

When your three minutes are over, count your nouns, and put the number on this line: _____

So, how many words do you have in your list? Three? Five? Ten?

Usually, it is from three to ten. Very seldom does someone in the audience have more than fifteen. Never in my practice has anyone had over thirty. When I ask why not thirty, forty, or one hundred, the usual answer is, "Not enough time." Is this what you thought?

Hmm . . . what you're saying is, "You, the author of the book, gave us too little time." So you are still "blaming it on the professor." Somebody is to be blamed again, right?

You're still not saying, "Oh, thirty, forty, one hundred? Is it possible? I'd like to know how to do it because I seem to be unable to, *yet*." But with an attitude of positiveness and openness, you *will* be able to.

The phrase, "I would like to learn" is very different from the phrase, "It is your fault; just give me more time."

So it is time again to choose your position. If you prefer the position, "I want to know how to be more creative, and I am ready to learn more," then we can move on to analyzing your answers.

Have you chosen your position? Ready?

Let me try to guess your first noun. Was it *lemon*? For the majority of people it is *lemon*. It is round, sour, and yellow. What fits these three adjectives better? It is the first answer that comes to many minds. This demonstrates what makes us normal, usual, and traditional. It's understandable, as we all live in the same culture. We were likely educated in similar curriculums and, therefore, we tend to think the same.

Below, you'll see a ladder of solutions. Look at the ladder from the lowest steps. Where do your answers fall?

Mood (non-object, but since a mood can be "blue," it can also be yellow)
Angry man with jaundice—round face, yellow skin, sour face expression (metaphorically sour)
Bad car ("lemon"), VW Beetle that doesn't work (still an object, but metaphorically sour)
Tennis ball, dirty socks, yellow balloon under acid rain, (non-edibles, but still could be sour)
Vitamin, medicine pill, jawbreaker, cheese, cake (artificially produced edibles)
Lemon, apple, orange, tomato, spoiled squash, (all fruit and vegetables—naturally grown edibles)

This ladder also can be presented with one stick for every noun:

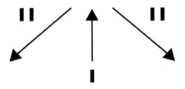

Here is the explanation of what happens in our minds. Our thinking moves in associations, so words like *round*, *yellow*, and *sour* are connected with other words. When our minds move in the same row of words (known as a *paradigm*), this association is called a *shift*.

If our thinking moves to another row or paradigm, the association is called a *transition*:

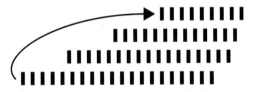

Finally, if the next move takes us over several paradigms, the association is called a *leap:*

When people hear the shift answers, there are no smiles; when people hear the *transition* associations, there is a general kind of "Yep"; and when people hear the *leap* solutions, there is silence first, and then laughter. By the way, all humor is built on the leaps. Good movies are built on leaps. Leaps stretch your mind and make you think.

This analysis is called *qualitative analysis.* We analyzed the quality of your answers. Now, from this qualitative analysis, we can go back to our quantitative analysis and explain why you didn't make twenty, thirty, or one hundred solutions.

We think in associations—from one thought to another, from a second thought to a third. Here is how a typical person thinks when responding to the previous exercise:

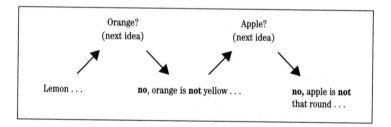

Orange? (next idea)   Apple? (next idea)

Lemon . . .   **no,** orange is **not** yellow . . .   **no,** apple is **not** that round . . .

Is that how you responded? If so, that is why your number of solutions was so small. You said "no" to your ideas.

Let me use an analogy. Imagine yourself driving a car. You press the accelerator, then the brake, then the accelerator, then the brake, and so on. How far will you get using this approach? In a scene from the movie *Twins,* the big twin (Arnold Schwarzenegger), presses pedals in this manner, and his car goes, stops, goes, stops, until his twin brother (Danny DeVito) tells him to use only one foot. Then, his car moves as it should.

So when your mind produces an idea and then says "no" to it, it is just like stomping on the accelerator and then on the brake. The result? A lot of jerking and little distance covered.

In 1937, Alex Osborn invented brainstorming. You probably know the rules: withhold criticism, accept all ideas. You've probably used brainstorming at work or in school many times while working in groups. No doubt you withheld criticism of your group members, and together you worked toward creative ideas and solutions.

Why not grant yourself the same positive support, the same generosity and latitude that you give to others? If there is group brainstorming, there must be individual brainstorming. Withhold self-criticism. If you reject your ideas, you give yourself no foundation from which to leap to even better ideas. Embrace your ideas. Use them as platforms from which to leap.

THE SECOND LAW OF MEGACREATIVITY

The main cause for low performance lies in the word *no*. *No* and *not* are harmful words. They are harmful tactically, strategically, mentally, and emotionally.

To increase your creativity, learn to avoid *no* and *not*.

The law that expresses it in a special way is, *Why Not Every (K)not?*

This is the Second Law of MegaCreativity. It means that when you hear *no* or *not* in your own thoughts and words or in somebody else's, you have to ask, "Why not?" The "(k)not" part of the law looks strange on purpose. I want to emphasize that every *not* in your thinking is like a knot—it ties you, it restricts you, it does not allow you to go forward, just as it happened in the exercise with *round, sour,* and *yellow.*

Now, for practice, when I say a phrase containing *no* or *not,* your task will be to say, "Why not?" Say it aloud and also write it.

It's **not** doable! _____

It's **not** possible! _____

No one did it in life! _____

It is **not** the way we do things here. _____

Nobody tried this, and you won't (won't = will **not**—

a hidden *not*). _____

Do**n't** even think of it (don't = do **not**—a hidden

not). _____

Nothing is available (combined *no*). _____

Nowhere to go (combined *no*). _____

Nobody can do it (combined *no*). _____

It is **not** feasible. _____

It is **not** for you! _____

If you have said, "Why not?" it at least ten times, you will more quickly recognize *no* and *not* in speech and you will be able to respond properly. When you hear yourself thinking "I cannot," you will correct yourself by saying "Why not?"

Before moving on, let me note three exceptions to the Second Law.

The Second Law cannot be used if the expression deals with:

- social laws or legal domain
- morality
- ethics or rules of behavior

For example, the law tells us not to kill or steal. It would be wrong to ask, "Why not?" In almost every case (with notable and usually comical exceptions), laws are there to protect us from each other and ourselves. Remember that creativity is meant to advance society for the good of all people. Laws are the result of creativity. They allow us a great deal of freedom and protect us at the same time. Creating laws and maintaining them is creativity, too—it is called *humane creativity*. [For details, please see my article in the *Encyclopedia of Creativity* (Academic Press, 1999).]

Another exception involves morality systems. If a morality system states, "You shall not commit adultery," it would be wrong to ask, "Why not?" The third exception involves ethics (rules of behavior). If a rule says, "Do not drive on the left side of the road," you'd better listen because the first truck going in your direction will prove you wrong. These rules may differ depending on the country or culture. In Singapore, for instance, it is the opposite: "Do not drive on the *right* side of the road."

These laws exist to maintain a sense of order—of civilization. Without them, we'd still be out bashing one another on the head with stones in order to defend a cave.

Thinking *No* Makes You a No-Thinker

Let's apply the Second Law of MegaCreativity to our problem of *yellow, sour,* and *round.*

- Can a chair be yellow, sour, and round? Yes.
- Can a table be yellow, sour, and round? Yes.
- Can a wall be yellow, sour, and round? Yes.
- Can a building be yellow, sour, and round? Yes.

Seemingly everything can be yellow, sour, and round. So let's ask ourselves what can*not* be yellow, sour, and round. When I ask this question in my seminars, there usually is a pause before somebody says, "A square."

I like this answer. It means that people are thinking, "A square cannot be round." And here is again the difference between a normal (closed by norms) mind and a creative (open) mind. "The problem," I say, "is not in the reality. The problem is still in your mind. It is you who says 'cannot.' In nature everything is possible. Round squares? They are everywhere."

- Many city *squares* in Bombay are *round.* (They use rotaries instead of traffic lights.) Read it again: ". . . squares . . . are round."
- Boxers fight in a roped square, but it is called a ring (rings are round).

Can you think of other examples of round squares? If you consciously step over the *no* in your mind, then instead of looking for objections, you will find many other cases of round squares. When you ask yourself, "Why not?" you force your brain to step over the line of negation and search for an explanation. When you say "no," you block yourself from moving to a possibly great idea. As a result, you feel frustrated, you feel stupid, and your self-esteem goes down. The chain is so simple. Avoid it! Allow yourself creativity and creative thinking! Allow your mind to open. If you still have difficulties, look at the list below.

My small collection of round squares now includes the following:

• If you wrap a square handkerchief around a tennis ball, it will be a round square. Every day we see square napkins rolled into roundness next to our dinner plates.

• If you squeeze a square piece of paper into a ball, it will be a round square.

• In nature, everything is curved. Straight lines and squares are abstracts invented by the human mind. We fall victim to our own inventions. We tend to think that abstracts like squares exist. Actually, every square is formed by four tops. No matter how precise they are, they can have only one molecule at the peak. These molecules are round. It would be very difficult to find a square molecule or atom.

• The same is true about a square as a drawn geometric figure. The sharpest corner ends up with a dot, and a dot is round. So every square is round (or at least rounded).

• My friend made a picture of several small boxes revolving on the perimeter of a large circle.

• My friend's second version is a square made up of circles.

• My next version is based on the fifth item. It is a square rotating at great speed. An observer sees a circle. So, it is a round square.

• One more idea: A balloon or any circle folded in the form of a square is round but square. A packed parachute is closer to being a square than to being round. It becomes round when it opens. By the way, this is a nice analogy. Surely you have heard the phrase, "Minds are like parachutes: They work best when they are open." An open mind is like a parachute. An open mind is like a round square! Ha-ha!

Understand that the number of round squares in this world is infinite. List more round squares on the following lines:

_____

_____

_____

_____

_____

_____

Now try some other lists. Try "black whiteness." Try "dry liquid." Try "tender roughness." Remember the First and Second laws as you make your lists. Use the lists to practice and master these laws.

When I explain to some people the concept of avoiding *no*, they begin to argue. "How about children? We still have to say 'no' to them if they ask for something we cannot afford."

Well, while explaining the drawbacks of *no*, I said to avoid *no* and *not*—they are destructive. However, I did not say you have to agree with everything. Disagree, but in positive terms. Use positive words. For example, when you see a child ready to jump from the table, instead of saying "Don't jump!" what would you say?

Here are some examples to follow:

- "Stay there, I am coming, and I will catch you."
- "Wait! I am coming!"
- "If you jump, you can hurt yourself."

There are hundreds of ways to say "no" without using the word *no*. So to return to the first task of the chapter, if you said "no" to the offer to write a definition of creativity, please reconsider it now. Say "Why not?" to your earlier "no," and make the definition.

Learn to say "yes" to possibilities as well as to impossibilities, to probabilities and improbabilities. Say "Why not?" and try.

Chapter Five

Launch to MegaCreativity

> Everything that looks great now, once seemed
> impossible.
>
> CHINESE PROVERB

By making the leaps we discussed in the previous chapter, you can dramatically increase the speed with which you generate ideas. You are on your way to MegaCreativity, but let's step back for a moment to determine what we mean by *creativity*. Think of every creative process as accelerating something, making it better and faster. If we think of creativity in this way, we can determine whether or not a process is truly creative. Consider these examples:

• Natural conception and delivery of a child is not creativity; however, speeding up this process, or creating life in vitro, which increases the natural rate of conception and delivery, is creativity.

• Natural dissemination of seeds by plants for reproduction is not creativity; however, toiling and fertilizing the soil for a higher harvest, and thereby increasing the speed at which products are produced, is creativity.

• Natural beauty is not creativity; however, a beautician's work is creativity because it either accelerates the natural process of maturing or slows the natural process of aging.

• Natural production of meaningful sounds (for instance, the sound you make when you are pushed, kicked, or scared) is not creativity; however, artificially speeding up the production of meaningful sounds (speech and language, as well as music) is certainly creativity.

• Natural flying (as with birds and insects) is not creativity; however, man-made flying machines are examples of creativity because they increase the natural speed of moving.

• Naturally occurring teaching (for instance, by example, as it is done in the animal world) is not creativity; however, artificially speeding up the process of teaching (designing programs, schools, props) is creativity—that is what I call *educational creativity.*

• Naturally developing life (biological level) and inner life (psychological level) is not creativity; however, the process of acceleration in shaping somebody's character is creativity.

In support of the last point, I often use the words of Etty Hillesum, who said, "It is possible to create, even without ever writing a word or painting a picture, by simply molding one's inner life. And that too is a deed." It is because we create our lives, too—we are either accelerating events (achievements) or procrastinating and slowing our own growth. Our lives are the result of our creativity, whether we call it a "creative stance," as does Sid Parnes, or "self-actualization," as does Abraham Maslow.

From this point of view, decide which of the following processes are creative or may be creative:

- cooking
- painting
- doodling
- sewing
- writing
- scribbling
- plowing
- working at a conveyor belt
- collecting berries
- collecting stamps
- reading
- spelling
- running
- flying
- swimming

Every action listed above can be a creative process. It can be less creative or more creative, but somebody invented cooking, painting, doodling, sewing, scribbling, plowing, and they all accelerated our natural speed. Even processes as natural as running can be creative: skate running, running for no purpose, running for president, etc.

With this new vision of creativity, it becomes clear that the value and number of creative acts can be measured and the intensity or efficiency of the creative process can be measured. With all these numerical factors being measured, we also know that creative output can be increased.

However, before we go to these levels, let's do the job we know we can do.

NATURAL THINKING

In my seminars, before we begin to work on MegaCreativity, I usually give students a task to invent something new, like a pen or pens. I allow them to work for five to ten minutes. Now it's your turn. Please invent a pen or pens.

After five to ten minutes, how many new pens did you manage to invent?

When I ask this question, students are often surprised because I didn't ask them to invent as many pens as they could. They have the right to be confused. We retrace my instructions, and they recall that I said "a pen or pens." I left the amount up to them, and the majority created only one. Some students are proud to show three versions. If at least one person somehow has five or seven, I am truly happy. They think, however, that they have achieved good quality, so we listen to some of the different pen descriptions. They are interesting. I praise the students, and I promise to return to the quality issue later. I also remind them that the First Law is Quit Quitting, so there must be as many solutions as possible. Quantity first! It is not an accident that it is named the "First" Law. All the rest, including the quality, comes second.

My students (and you) know how difficult it is to generate an original idea. You also know that the process of thinking takes time. This particular case was an example of *natural thinking*. Natural thinking is creative. Some researchers say that intellect as a whole is the ability to solve problems creatively. However, the rate of creativity in this or that particular case can differ greatly. So let me state it again: A person can be more creative or less creative but not creative or noncreative. The same person can be less creative in one situation and more creative in another situation. Creativity is rather a degree of ingenuity and originality than something permanent that is attached to thinking.

When you take away the absoluteness of creative/non-creative, it becomes a matter of how to teach people to be more creative rather than how to make them creative. The same is true about innovative thinking, which we will discuss later.

When the question is how to increase somebody's creativity, then the counterquestion is: How much do you want to increase your creativity? Would you like to double it? Triple it? Increase it ten times? What is your dream? To become a little bit more creative? Or to become everything you can be?

The average person can create one to ten ideas in ten minutes (this is from $\frac{1}{10}$ to one idea per minute); talented people can make ten ideas per minute (especially if asked to do as much as possible); a genius hypothetically can create one hundred ideas per minute. That doesn't mean the genius really makes that many ideas, but her thinking makes leaps and bounds.

I promise that you will make one million ideas per minute. Do you trust me? As a rule, many people do not: They shake their heads and say "no!" If you belong in this group of people, I'm sorry to hear that. You broke the Second Law of MegaCreativity. What do you have to say when you hear this "no" in your thinking?

"Why not?"

Good. Now we can move to the exercise that will *prove* it to you.

MAKING ONE MILLION IDEAS PER MINUTE

There are about two hundred methods and techniques you can use to increase the quantity and the quality of your ideas. Some methods would increase the number of ideas a little bit; the others would lead you to the top. Would you like to see the world from the top? Would you like to see how the world looks from a mountain peak or from a satellite?

I will show you a methodology called BAMMA (Brain Attack Multiplied by Morphological Analysis) that leads to MegaCreativity, but I will need your help.

First, list the parts of a pen. Then place them vertically in a list. Make sure there are at least ten parts listed (for making the later calculations easier). Use the following table as an example.

ball		
ink		
body		
cap		
tip		
spring		
clip		
cartridge		
belt		
grip		

Second, fill the table by brainstorming different ideas that come from each element, but do each element separately. For example, for the ball, the following features might come to mind, which you would list in the row: plastic ball, glass ball, square ball (what a leap!), triangle ball (why not?), graduation ball (another leap!), football, flying ball, wet ball, smooth ball, red ball. Be sure that there are at least ten of these characteristics.

Some of the features, like "square ball," may look strange. However, the ball in the pen is just a device through which ink goes to paper—it doesn't *have* to be round. Practically, the word *ball* is already limiting your imagination. (This is a language, or semantic, barrier to overcome.) This "writing device" may be in the form of a box, a ratchet—whatever. Just imagine an artistic pen with a ratchet that releases a striped line of ink. What an improvement it could be for graphic artists. After all, we went from quill to ball; why limit it now?

When you're close to the tenth feature in the row, ask yourself whether it is possible to have a pen without any ball. When people say "yes," I make a special column at the right side of the table and write 0 (zero) there. It means the zero option of the ball—the ball is absent.

Keep in mind that this is a simple brainstorming technique, but you do it separately for every element of the matrix (table). If you have problems generating ideas, take another technique—for instance, the random-word technique—and fill in the row with random words from the dictionary or any other book at hand. Most people continue the idea generation process until the table looks like the example below.

ball	plastic, glass, square, triangle, graduation, foot, flying, wet, smooth, red	0
ink	dry, smelling, erasable, poisonous, Inc., invisible, alcohol, pink, jet, frozen	0
body	built, car, of laws, hand-formed, flexible, rubber, telescopic, changeable, toy, any (like in *anybody*, *somebody*)	0
cap	football, metal, secret, captain's, transparent, radioactive, needle, tooth, box, child's	0
tip	silver, crystal, reading, three-dollar, rhombic, wooden, smart, jelly, ultrasound, rusty	0
spring	air, oval, late, early, blossoming, forest, flower, Canada, combustion	0
clip	decorated, iron, converted, Velcro, radio, video, money, hair, crab, delta, elastic	0
cartridge	edible, cylinder, rifle, X ray, laser, film, perfume, lipstick, whiskey, truncated	0
belt	blinking, coding, karate, slacks, earth, asteroid, cucumber, cute, screen, page	0
grip	slimy, soft, grippe, computer, paste, ethical, violin, liquid, family, eye	0

After you complete the matrix, you begin your selective synthesis. Try to combine various features into a single pen. Make a variety of combinations. Students are often surprised to see that everything fits. The invented combinations and, therefore, versions of the pen might look like this:

- square ball
- poisonous ink
- changeable body
- needle cap

- three-dollar tip
- late spring
- video clip
- lipstick cartridge
- asteroid belt
- eye grip

Some people have problems envisioning a three-dollar tip pen, but think of it this way: Every pen is sold with three dollars attached to it, or when the tip at a restaurant is over three dollars, a special pen is included as a token of appreciation to the customer. In the same manner, imagine the video clip, asteroid belt, and so on. The main rule here is to not discard any feature—just invent a new pen or two for any new combination.

Finally, when you have produced enough pens to impress yourself, check the originality of your pens. Has anybody seen a pen like the one described in the previous example? Definitely, no one has seen such a pen, so the quality of newness is high.

During my classes, we certainly do not go to the patent library; we just visualize the pens, and we use our group knowledge (as if this is global knowledge) to determine whether this or that pen is available in the world. We check several versions in the same manner—they are all of high newness quality. Truly, have you ever seen a pen with a square ball and an asteroid belt?

Look for the best version out of all that you have. After asking my students to name the best version, I point to the column of all zeroes, and I say, "Don't you think the best pen will be the one with no ball, no ink, no body, no cap . . . the pen having nothing and still writing?" After some search for examples, they agree. This is the moment I introduce the so-called Ideal Final Result (IFR)—the concept of extreme heuristic (discovering) power. Genrikh S. Altshuller introduced the concept to help people find the best possible results in inventing. In short, the IFR is an idea of the zero mechanism that nevertheless fulfills the needed functions. It looks like the functions are fulfilled by themselves. No mechanism is required. You need something—it is done! You travel without cars or planes: teleportation. You communicate without shouting, without flags, without Morse code: Press the button, speak, done. Not ideal yet! There is a button. But close to it. Altshuller also showed that all technical systems evolve in the direction of IFR because every next improved machine or mechanism increases the "ideality" of the system.

The history of writing shows it vividly. The earliest known writing systems that survived in history are stone inscriptions. Do you think it was easy or difficult to write with a stone chisel on stone? The next system of writing used special sticks to press the images of letters onto soft clay tablets. Was it easy? Slaves were probably molding the clay for the masters to write messages. Writing on tree bark, on animal skin, and on cloth marked the next steps. Knives for cutting as well as special paints for marking still kept writing a privilege of the wealthy. Papyrus and ink appeared after that, and the process of writing became less laborious. Paper made it even more accessible, but it still required a lot of handwriting skill. Different handwriting was difficult to read. Then came typewriters, and poor handwriting was not a problem. However, if one made a mistake, it was difficult to correct, and it was impossible to move around paragraphs or sentences. As a solution, word processors and computers appeared. Good, but they require typing, which some people hate. The next step was voice recognition. Now people can speak and the computer types it. Heavens! Do you see the movement to the IFR in writing? Less work, faster results. So what is the next step? Right! Why should we dictate at all? It takes time and energy. The next step is thought recognition. No equipment, no apparatus, no special machines, no writing or typing required, but the end result is written, or the function of writing is fulfilled.

For us, the IFR is vividly shown by the zero column on the table. Students have a lot of fun trying to find the IFR for the pen.

TAKING THE LEAP TO MEGACREATIVE THINKING

While working on the table, you were making a leap to MegaCreative thinking. Here is how.

How many new pens do we have in this matrix? Some people say one hundred, some people say more. Very seldom do I get the right answer. The number of versions is equal to the number of combinations, meaning it is factorial. Look at it: Every feature of every element can be combined with the other features. One click, or one change, makes a hundred different varieties. Moreover, a pen may have minimum features (down to zero = IFR) or all of the features. It means that theoretically, there may be a pen with all one hundred features, or even all one hundred features in one element, if we choose to rotate columns as well as rows. Can you imagine a pen with a ball that has a video, a radio, a computer, lip coloring, and that stays transparent and is edible? It'd be useful, no doubt! One of my volunteer editors gives me a hard time by writing in the margin, "Edible ball sounds almost crazy." Good! The crazier the better! I like crazy ideas. Moreover, for an idea to be a genius idea, it must be a little bit crazy. That's why Albert Einstein said, "If at first the idea is not absurd, then there is no hope for it."

Let's explore the versions you can make from an edible ball. There are several possible applications here. Children, for instance, like to bite their pens when they write. Bad habit! One could try to correct this bad habit by using bitter-tasting edibles. An edible ball could sit at the top of the pen; when children bite the pens, they taste pepper or mustard. This is edible, but it tastes awful. As a result, after a couple of accidental bites, the habit disappears. The second version is to have some medicine in the pen ball. The third version is to have a high-calorie food hidden in the pen ball for spies to use in case of emergencies (hunger, no food to survive, etc.). Is that enough craziness?

Now back to the number of versions produced by the table. In mathematics, the number of combinations is calculated by factorials and is shown as $n!$. For example, the factorial of 4 is equal to the product of $4 \times 3 \times 2 \times 1 = 24!$ When written mathematically, it looks like this: $4! = 24$. It means that the number of combinations out of 4 elements equals 24.

Let's look at the factorials of small numbers first to

see the speed of growth. Factorial of 6, or when mathematically expressed, $6! = 720$. Factorial of 7, or $7! = 5,040$.
Factorial of 8, or $8! = 40,320$. Factorial of 9, or $9! = 362,880$.
Factorial of 10, or $10! = 3,628,800$. See how the numbers
grow? Factorial of 10 is already more than three million.
The highest factorial my computer gives is factorial of 15,
or $15! = 1,307,674,368,000$.

The matrix we have built includes 10 (vertical) $\times$ 10
(horizontal) $= 100$ items. How can you calculate the number of combinations out of 100 items? This number or
$100! = 9.332621544394e + 157$. Whatever it means, it is far
beyond twenty or thirty million because even the factorial
of 15 is in the trillions. Frankly speaking, this is overkill.
It is enough that only 11 elements will produce over thirty
million combinations because $11! = 39,916,800$. However,
for the simplicity of the process (and we are not greedy
at all), let's consider that we have produced *only*
30,000,000 combinations!

So, if you've been working for thirty minutes, the efficiency of your work will be equal to thirty million ideas
(or combinations): thirty minutes $=$ one million ideas/min-
ute (30,000,000 ideas: 30 min $= 1,000,000$ ideas/min.). Consequently, you would have been producing a million ideas
a minute.

This is MegaCreativity!

Achieving such a level makes you a MegaCreator and
your mind a MegaCreative mind! Congratulations!

Okay, let's do it again for another object. I will choose
a table lamp. Help me. What do we do first?

Cut it mentally into pieces.

Good. What are the lamp parts?

Lamp stand, lamp base, clicker, bulb, wire, shade . . .

List it all in a table.

stand		
base		
clicker		
bulb		
wire		
shade		

Now what's next?

We have to brainstorm each of them (and have fun doing it).

Okay. Let's do it.

stand	newsstand, apart, nightstand, morning stand, stand strike, still, steal, steel	
base	Air Force, stolen, building, liquid, acid, BASE (British Aeronautic Sleeping Equipment), sitting	
clicker	mouse, ant, beetle (do it by yourself—enjoy)	
bulb	tulip (do it by yourself—practice)	
wire	money . . .	
shade		

When we finish the table, what do we do next?

We check the newness of the variants.

All right. Let's do it. A lamp that stands up when you strike at the table (strike stand), and has a liquid-filled base (oh, it could be beautiful), with a beetle swimming in this liquid, and sending a signal to a tulip bulb to blossom, and sending some money to the bank every time you . . . touch the wire. Is it new?

It sure is.

How many versions do we have here? Depending on how you finished the table, find the number of words in it. Is it twenty or thirty? Then make it twenty or thirty factorial! This will be a huge number of combinations.

If you want an additional round of practice, here is another table. Choose the object to invent and make a table of your own. Harvest the results. Have fun.

You can use this method to generate ideas or solutions on any topic, but I would wait until you become comfortable with unrelated objects (at least ten times) before trying a work-related topic. Work-related thinking is often too deeply entrenched in our minds, and ideas look too connected to reality. We have to move away and train our minds in this new process. Only then can we move back and apply these new strategies to old problems. This is how geniuses work. Why do you think Einstein liked to play the violin?

When you have mastered this specially structured thought process, you will be able to produce more than a million new ideas per minute. Therefore, you will be a MegaCreator. The process works, but you must practice it to become proficient and practice it even more to become a master. Still, if you have worked through the examples in this chapter, you are on your way to achieving MegaCreativity. Now you also have a better understanding of BAMMA (Brain Attack Multiplied by Morphological Analysis): We use brainstorming, or brain attack, but we multiply its power by the table. We brainstorm the separate parts and then multiply the options.

PROOF FOR DOUBTING MINDS

Some people still say, "But I thought we would be making one million a minute, just one idea after another."

The following exercise, based on a well-known story, should help eliminate such doubts. One day about two centuries ago, a math teacher came into class and, probably wishing to sit quietly for an hour, gave his fourth-graders the task to add all numbers from 1 to 100. How surprised he was when one of the boys came up to him in five minutes and turned in a correct answer. How was this possible? The boy surely was a genius. Let's find out by trying it ourselves. Please, take a sheet of paper and add all numbers from 1 to 100 in five minutes.

After five minutes, look at your results. They differ depending on individuals' math skills, but very seldom is the result correct. The answer is 5,050. By the way, the name of the student who did it was Karl Gauss. Yes, the same Gauss who later became a famous mathematician and a physicist, the same Gauss who touched with his genius hand nearly every branch of physics. You've probably heard about demagnetizing, or degaussing, ships, tapes, and even our TV screens. Furthermore, the unit of intensity of magnetic fields is called the gauss.

Now back to the puzzle. What did you do? How did

you start? You probably began to add numbers like this: $1+2+3+4+5+6+7. \ldots$ Or in another version, you may have started from 100: $100+99+98+97. \ldots$

That is what I call the sequential mentality (working in sequence, one after another). We see the numbers, and we begin to work with them as we see them or as the teacher told to us. This often leads either to a very long process or to numerous mistakes.

A quick example of such modus operandi is another puzzle, $2+2\times2$. What is your answer?

The answer I most often hear is 8. The correct answer is 6 because we have to multiply first (the order of operations rule). In other words, the problem $2+2\times2$ must be solved as $2\times2=4$ and only after that $2+4=6$. The mistake is trivial, but it shows that despite learning and using the rules, the human brain often chooses the path of least resistance—sequential thinking. A genius brain acts differently. It does not begin to add $2+2$ as it is given in the sequences, but rather sees the situation as a whole and then starts with multiplication (according to the order of operations rule).

So when given the task to add numbers from 1 to 100, young Gauss looked at the situation from above . . .

1 2 3 4...   ...97 98 99 100

. . . and found that 1 and 100 make 101, 2 and 99 make 101, 3 and 98 make 101, and so on. His next move was to determine how many pairs like that were available in the sequence from 1 to 100. The answer was simple: 50 $(100 \div 2)$. So the sum of all numbers from 1 to 100 is $101 \times 50 = 5{,}050$. That is why Gauss solved the problem in five minutes. Five minutes of genius thinking are worth an hour or more of habitual sequential calculating. Moreover, Gauss created the method of calculating the sums, which uses multiplication instead of addition. Much faster! An algebraic formula for all calculations like that is the following:

$$X = (n = 1)(n : 2) = \frac{(n+1)n}{2}$$

(where n equals the final number in the sequence)

The same effect happens with our MegaCreativity. We do not reach it in a sequential manner. Instead, we reach it in a leap, and after the achieved result is recalculated into minutes, it gives us the million-fold increase. Like Gauss, view the situation from above, and then you'll understand MegaCreativity. Moreover, if our two-dimensional matrix is redone into a three-dimensional matrix, it is even more powerful than that, not to mention four, five, six, and more dimensions. Who knows in how many dimensions a true genius thinks?

SIX CENTURIES OF HISTORY

When we are finished with calculations and with doubting moods, I ask students to guess when these methods of thinking were invented. Students are surprised to learn that the history of the method starts with the medieval scholar Raymond Lully, who described it in his *Ars Magna*

(The Great Art) in the 1300s. In the twentieth century, Fritz Zwicky rediscovered the method and called it the "Morphological Approach."

There are variations to this approach. Some researchers begin from the outside, build the categories on the entrances to the table, and then converge to the inner cells. This version of the matrix is called the *convergent approach* (*con-* means "with, together," so *convergent* means "coming together"). It starts with categories on the outer dimensions of the matrix and then projects the meaning of these categories onto the cells inside the table. In BAMMA, I use a divergent version of the matrix. I prefer the divergent approach because (1) it has only one entrance (not three), (2) it doesn't make a box (are we going out of one box only to get into another?), and (3) rather than imploding, it explodes from the inside to the outside.

I was shown the BAMMA version by my teachers in creativity, V. Sigalov and A. Romanov, at the Institute of Inventive Creativity in Baku, Azerbaijan. This version, the inventors' version, looks like an opportunity missed by many. As a matter of fact, even specialists in creativity are surprised when I show them my matrix. Moreover, none of them ever used it for the purpose of calculating the efficiency of creative thinking and for achieving the highest levels. That is why it's called the discovery of Mega-Creativity—the discovery of the phenomenon and the ability of the human mind to generate over a million ideas per minute. You can use this version of the matrix for any field or activity—not just inventions. The process is practically the same.

I have nothing to hide from my students, so I also tell them that some researchers have a negative opinion of morphological analysis. Others devote books to it. I pay credit to everybody who helped develop the method since the fourteenth century. My role in this development is only discovering that it can be used for achieving the highest possible efficiency of creativity, which I call MegaCreativity, GigaCreativity, and even InfiCreativity that can be called AbsoluteCreativity. I also show that this method and the like can be used to train MegaCreators and Mega-Innovators, or, in simple terms, geniuses.

So if you practiced MegaCreativity two to three times, you discover that it's simple. Some people say, "Oh, it is too simple!" Yes, it is simple after somebody discovered it, just like adding sequential numbers became simple after Gauss discovered it or navigating to America became simple after Columbus discovered it. Genius things *are* simple . . . after they are discovered.

You just had an opportunity to see how two laws of MegaCreativity—Quit Quitting and Why Not Every (K)not?—lead you to peaks and horizons never before seen. Are you ready for more?

Chapter Six

Find the Essence

Genius is an ability to see through to the essential.

UNKNOWN AUTHOR

In this chapter, you'll learn the most important skill for a genius: finding the essence. For this purpose, we will use two methods: creating a definition and testing a definition by counter examples. Then, you will learn how to find the essence of a task, situation, or problem and learn how to discover solutions. Seeing the essence is essential to becoming a genius.

Tools like BAMMA (Brain Attack Multiplied by Morphological Analysis) train only one ability—the ability to generate multiple ideas. The quality and depth of these ideas are also important. It is not easy to become a genius creator.

What is in this peak of human mental capacity?

If we are trying to find the nature of genius thinking, one feature is immediately obvious: Genius is an ability to see through to the essential. A genius has a special way of seeing things—all at once, all together, and all the way to the core. A genius is able to create the essence from split and isolated parts of the whole. A genius is able to understand the essence without always having all the information.

Essence, as I'll use it, is opposite to the concept of *phenomenon*. On the surface, there are billions of landscapes and visions, millions of colors, and thousands of different sensations. These elements comprise phenomena. Phenomena are diverse and can be misleading. Out of this enormous variety, a genius chooses the most important aspects, called the *essence*. Somehow phenomena are transparent for geniuses and opaque for other people.

For example, people can be of all colors, shapes, weights, and ages, but they are all people. The essence is the same; phenomena are different. Another example: With all the varieties of trees, bushes, birds, and flowers, your brain still fixes them as trees (apple, maple, pine), bushes (mulberry, curry), birds (eagle, sparrow, duck), and flowers (rose, tulip, forget-me-not). Essence does not exist as itself. There is no such thing as a generic flower or a generic tree. There are roses, daffodils, and irises, and there are oak trees, maple trees, and birch trees. However, the essence expressed in the words *flower* and *tree* is common for all of them. The essence is present in each item, but it does not exist as itself.

Here is a simple example of how difficult it is to see the essence in life, work, and education. I approached a school principal with the promise to help his most problematic children. The principal probably considered me a salesperson and said at once, "I have a lot to do today. I do not have time for your program." And he really was busy. There were a lot of papers on his desk. The school was on "caution status" (it just barely left the "alert status"). What does this principal see? He sees the surface of things, not the essence.

The essence of his work is children, so making them better is his direct duty. The program that he had no time to see was titled A Genius in Every Child; a variant of the program is titled Genius. In two days it saves those children who, as teachers say, "cannot be helped," those who are doomed to drugs, violence, jail, prostitution, teen pregnancy, and early death. The program also dramatically changes the teachers' vision. After the program, they understand there is a genius in every child, and they begin to teach differently.

The principal in Alabama was rejecting this program without even seeing it. So I asked him, "What is the *essence* of your work: time, building, papers, funds, parents, or children?" He gazed at me for a moment. "Children," he answered slowly. "So if I save ten to twenty of your 'most troubled' children, and show teachers how to work with them, and help you get out of this caution status, would you be interested?" This time there was no pause. "When can we start?" he asked at once. As a result, one hour and twenty minutes later, the principal was laughing and wanted to have all his teachers reeducated. He also began to see the essence: Children are of value. Every child may be a future genius. That is what our modern public school educators often do not see. They see money, funds, papers, and tests. The child, with his or her "unique bent of a genius" (as Plato said), the child as the essence of the system, is lost.

Finding an essence is a labor. It requires skill and persistence. Geniuses become skilled in this activity, and one day they see through to the essence, and they do it faster than other people. The search for essence is difficult, but there are special exercises to help. We will practice two of these exercises here.

DEFINING THINGS

In my classes, I have students define a simple item such as a table or a bike. Here is our typical dialogue:

Table? It's a wooden plate on four legs.

Wooden? Can it be plastic? Iron? Glass?
Yes. Sorry. It would be better to say a flat surface on four legs.

Okay. You say four legs. Are there tables with three legs?
Yes . . .

Are there tables with two legs?
Yes . . .

Are there tables with one leg?
Yes . . .

So the number of legs doesn't matter. The number of legs, as a characteristic, seems unnecessary for the table. Right?
Right.

Good. Let's go further. Are there tables with no legs?
Yes . . . no . . .

Well, are there tables attached to the wall?
Yes.

So they have no legs. How about hanging tables?
Yes . . . we didn't think about those.

Therefore, the parameter of legs is not necessary at all. Right?
Right.

So what is left? Flat surface? Did you say flat surface?
Yes.

Well. The wall is a flat surface. Is it a table?
No (embarrassed) . . . We meant a horizontal surface.

Horizontal? Sometimes tables are a little tilted, so horizontal as a characteristic is not always true. Also, the floor is a horizontal surface. The ceiling is a horizontal surface. Are they tables?
No (laughing) . . .

So what is left from your definition?
Nothing.

It means that the first definition contained no necessary features. Let's go back. You certainly know that definitions are supposed to define the essence. So what is the essence of the table?
. . . (silence) . . .

Well, the essence must include the necessary and sufficient characteristics of the object for people to understand it from the definition. Also, remember the rule: When trying to define things, first go up to the next closest category on the ladder of abstraction (more specific categories are below, and more general categories are above). After going up to the next category, go down to separate the object within the category. Here is how it looks graphically:

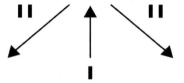

For example, if you are trying to define a poodle, what would you say?

A dog. A pet.

Well, if you say a pet, then it is too high in the category of abstraction because cats are pets, too. Parrots are pets. A fish is a pet, too. The ladder of abstraction for a poodle would look like this:

Objects

Live beings (because there are non-living beings)

Pets (because there are wild animals—not pets)

Dogs (because there are cats), birds, fish, etc.

Poodles (because there are terriers, pinchers, bull-dogs, etc.)

Saying that a poodle is a dog is good; "domestic dog" is even better because there are wild dogs like dingoes. From this higher category in the ladder of abstraction, go down to the other breeds of the dog and define what differentiates a poodle from a Doberman, a chow chow, and so on. Now let's go back to the table issue. What is a table? Where do you go first?

Up! It's a piece of furniture.

Good for you. In this one move you have cut off floors, ceilings, and walls. That was perfect! Now let's go down and to the sides to differentiate a table from the other pieces of furniture.

It's a piece of furniture with a horizontal surface on a certain level.

Better, but chairs and shelves have horizontal surfaces, too. Are they tables?

No.

Try again.

A chair is for sitting.

Hmm . . . I can sit on a table, too. However, that's an excellent attempt!

A table is bigger than a chair, and it's for tools.

Great! When you say "for" something you are going to the function of an object: A chair is for sitting. A table is for working, for holding and working with tools. A shelf is for holding only. So what is a table?

A piece of furniture for working with tools and for eating.

Excellent. Now compress this into a two- or three-word definition. What do you do with tools on the table? What does it help you to do?

Organize things and keep them ready for use.

Marvelous! Make it shorter!

Work space-organizing furniture piece.

Wow! Compare your first definitions with the last definition. What a difference! Do you see it?

Oh, yes!

That is the difference between the trivial, or phenomenal, definition—plastic, legs, surface, and all the other unimportant things—and the genius, or essence, definition. Was it easy to get to the essence?

No, it was difficult.

Sure, it's difficult. But if you could train yourself to give definitions like that, do you think people would consider you a genius?

They certainly would.

So, your fate is in your hands (actually, in your mind). Train yourself to give definitions like that. Later, we will learn one more technique—mastering your ability to see through to the essential. When a genius gets to the guts of things, everything becomes simple and obvious. That's why genius solutions are usually high on the scale of abstraction, or on the scale of specific/general.

We will further train this type of vision later, but for now let's use your new skills of visualizing and thinking.

Finding the essence, as you saw in the example of the table, is eliminating the unnecessary and selecting the necessary features or aspects. All the selected necessary aspects must be sufficient for the essence. A table is a *work space* organizer not a rest space organizer (bed) and not an auxiliary space organizer (shelf). Finally, a table is a work space *organizer,* not a work space protector (cover) and not a work space illuminator (lamp). Only include necessary and sufficient characteristics—nothing more! Otherwise, the essence will transform into another essence, or it will become indistinguishable from the other essence.

TESTING THE DEFINITIONS

Now that you have the method for defining things, there must be a method of testing these definitions, or checking which one of them is correct. One of the most effective methods is the method of counter examples.

A story going back to ancient Greece tells us about the time when philosophers tried to define a man (or a human). Plato's definition, which was popular at the time, stated that a man was a two-legged animal with no feathers. Diogenes, who was famous for his sarcastic remarks and puzzling actions (for example, he lived in a bathtub at the city square), once brought to Plato's "school" a rooster whose feathers were pulled out. He threw this rooster into the yard where all of Plato's pupils were sitting around their teacher. While watching the rooster run around naked, he shouted with laughter, "Here is Plato's man!"

So your ability to find an example that debunks the definition, or proves it wrong, is a great ability to train and practice. Remember, in the dialogue about the table, I did nothing but provide you with counter examples. I said, "Are there tables with three legs?" Of course. And the definition about the table having four legs was proven wrong. I did it many times, and that led to the correct definition.

Look at how this process of finding the essence works for the example with the school principal and the educational system. Why do I think a child is the essence of the educational (teaching/learning) system? Let's test it quickly.

- If the principal or administrator is not available, can teaching/learning happen? In other words, is there teaching/learning without administrators? (Are there tables without legs?) Yes. Thus, an administrator is not essential for teaching/learning to happen.
- Can teaching/learning occur if the school building is not available? In other words, is there teaching/learning without buildings? Yes. So, the building is not essential.
- Can teaching/learning happen if the papers and exams aren't present? Yes. So, the papers and exams are not essential.
- Can teaching/learning occur if the teacher is not present? No. There must be a teacher (in some form). So, a teacher is essential.
- Can teaching/learning occur if the student is not available? No. So, the student is an absolute essence of the teaching/learning system.

The conclusion is simple: If there is no child (student), then there is no teaching or learning, no education, and no system. The child is the essence of the system.

Here is your chance. With the knowledge you gained while defining the table, testing the definition of a man, and finding the essence of education, can you find the essence of your work? Can you find the essence of your life? Can you find the essence of music, the essence of literature, the essence of creativity, the essence of genius?

With all your newly trained skills, remember: Your definition of creativity or a genius may be the best. You are the creator of your future. Your definition can cause thousands and millions of changes; thus, you can become a MegaCreator, a genius mentioned in millions of books, and a person remembered by millions of people and followed by millions of learners. This is the path to genius, and you are a genius in the making.

Go for a Million

... so we too might walk in the newness of life.

BIBLE, ROMANS 6:4

This section will help you learn to use the next necessary step in the notion of a genius—the concept of innovation. I will explain innovation as the main feature of genius, prove that we are all innovative, and show you how to increase your innovativeness to a level more powerful than that of a natural genius. In other words, in this step you will open your mind to incredible opportunities—to MegaInnovation.

Chapter Seven

Innovate

To innovate is not to reform.

EDMUND BURKE

This chapter will give you a simple scientific vision of
innovation and a testable and repeatable definition that
will help you break the barriers of the mundane. A scientific view is the shortest and most economic view. To get
to this level, you will use your ability to see through to
the essential and your ability to give definitions (both
learned in the previous chapters).

TRAIN YOUR BRAIN

Here is an exercise in imagination that Lois Duna (3M
Company) offered at the closing ceremony of the American Creativity Association Annual Convention in Saint
Paul, Minnesota. When I asked for permission to use this
exercise, Lois graciously agreed and gave me several more
handouts. I have to confess that I am a voracious collector
of everything that can bring creative development to children or adults. If you have some puzzles or tasks, please
send them to the School of Geniuses.

Here is the exercise:

You and your crew have been exploring the Delta Section of the Galaxy Ruecta some twelve thousand light
years from Earth. You see a class M (Earthlike) planet in

one of the nearby solar systems. Your science officer numbers this planet RD1-M5.

Since all class M planets are routinely explored, your ship lands on RD1-M5. The first thing you see is a most interesting animal. Draw this animal in the box below.

When you are finished drawing, check your fantasy by the following criteria. (I changed them a little. Sorry, Lois.)

1. If your animal has less or more than one head, give yourself a point.
2. If your animal has less or more than two arms, give yourself a point.

3. If your animal has less or more than two legs, give yourself a point.

4. If your animal has less or more than one tail, give yourself a point.

5. If your animal has less or more than two eyes, give yourself a point.

6. If your animal has less or more than two ears, give yourself a point.

7. If your animal has less or more than one nose, give yourself a point.

8. If your animal has some strange feature, such as a communicating device or a defense device, give yourself a point.

How many points did you get?

If you have eight points, you did well. You are pushing beyond your previous limitations in creativity. If you didn't earn eight points, you can continue to improve.

After you have learned the criteria, make your drawing again.

Now that you finished the second picture, is your alien animal different? Is it a one-eyed, two-headed, seven-legged monster? Did you make your alien invisible? Just kidding! Lois asked that, too. If your animal is still visible, then the previous questions probably predetermined your picture. The first drawing is determined by your imagination (former experience); the second drawing is predetermined by the questions because now you know how to get more points (your experience expanded by including these questions). And if there were a third drawing, I am sure you would do even better.

This game has no winners. It's just a game of self-development and self-evaluation. However, it feels good to know you scored high. I felt good because I got eight points on my first drawing when Lois introduced us to the game at the seminar. Here is a picture of two of my pages. I will explain how I got the points in the game and was ahead of the game even when Lois asked about an invisible animal (the second catch).

The page with a box (as given).

The flip side of the page with my animal.

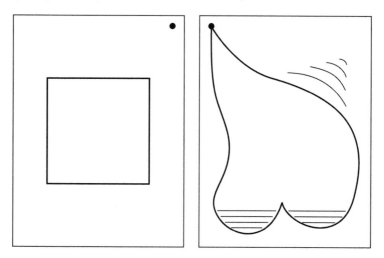

When the task was to draw an animal in the box, here is what I thought:

1. Why not get out of the box (as a given)? Where? To the corner. (So I made a dot in the corner of the first page.)
2. Why not get out of the sheet of paper as a given? Where? To the other side. (So I turned the sheet over.)
3. Why not get out of the animal look (as a given)? How? No legs, no arms, no head? As a sack? Formless? (So I made a vague form or shape.)

4. Why not get out of the traditional look (as implied by our culture)? How? I made a transparent animal that contains information in liquid (condensed) form. (So I made some liquid lines at the bottom.)

5. Why not get out of everything known (as implied by our knowledge)? How? I added some cute lines. Let the animal communicate positive feelings like enthusiasm from the upper membrane of the body (I added some waves from the right upper corner) and negative feelings like frustration from the left bottom corner (I did it the next time).

That is why I scored eight points at once. You also can see the five-step, runaway process—the process that takes your intellectual product far away from the norm and even ahead of possible catches. Force yourself to move five steps away from the task, and ask yourself "Why not?"

The second catch, as you remember, was whether your animal is invisible. My answer was yes because my animal was two-dimensional. You don't see the animal if you look at only one side of the paper (the first side); there is only a dot. You also don't see it when you look at the paper from the side (the paper looks like a thin line with nothing on it). From this exercise we see again the power of the first two laws of MegaCreativity as they apply to innovation.

NEWNESS AND INNOVATION

Linguistic analysis of the word *innovation* shows it is a pure sum of *in* + *nov* + *a[te]* + *tion*: [in]troduction of [nov]elty to the society by an active [-ate] process [-tion].

Actually, *innovation* is a lucky word. Not many words preserved their internal form in such a pure and transparent state. Linguists continue to argue about the majority of words. *Innovation* is an exception, maybe because it is young yet. Despite this obvious transparency, its interpretation is vague and varies greatly.

Some of the definitions state that innovation is creativity "implemented," "applied," or "realized." Some definitions state that innovation is creativity that brings "profit." Perhaps. Maybe all of the above; maybe none of the above.

Remember what we need for a definition? First eliminate all unnecessary elements. Use your ability to cut the unnecessary. Consider the following counter examples:

- A creative idea may be *implemented* into a machine, but the machine is getting rusty in the shed and is not shown to anybody. (Is this innovation?)
- A creative idea can be *applied* to achieve better results, but it is used individually—kept as a secret, or it is not even recognized as something valuable; so, it merely stagnates. (Is this innovation?)
- A creative idea can be *realized, actualized, materialized,* or whatever, and still be kept away from people. (Is this innovation?)

In any case, there is no innovation until it is shown to other people. The litmus paper for innovation is people, a social group, or, in general, society. If there is no "active process of introducing the newness into the society," it is not innovation yet.

So the basic feature of innovation is not implementation, not application, not realization, not actualization, and not materialization. It is the transition, the moment of transfer from the individual to a social group.

Creativity is the production of newness, and innovation is the consumption of newness by the society. In the simplest terms (just as we did it when defining the essence earlier), creativity is newness produced and innovation is newness transferred.

Both creativity and innovation are explained through one word: *newness*. It's not an accident. It's time to move deeper—to the basics, to the essence.

Before we do this, I'd like to ask you a question that I usually present in my university classes and business seminars.

"Would you eat the same food twice?"

Normally my students say, "Yes."

"Really?" I say. "But it has been digested. Would you like to eat it again?"

Confusion and looks of disgust come to the students' faces.

Then I explain: We can eat the same *type* of food, but not the same food. So we need new food (fresh). We also need new air (fresh) to breathe. People left without new air and new food would soon die because of lack of oxygen and nutrients.

From this small experiment, what do you see? Do people recognize newness? Some newness is strikingly visible, but some is not even noticed. Moreover, newness brings newness. A wheel makes it possible to make a cart. A cart makes it possible to invent an engine. An engine makes it possible to invent many other wheeled machines that have the ability to move. Some newness can cause minor change, while some can cause millions of changes. A genius would go for the latter—a newness that would cause millions of other newnesses to appear.

By the way, newness, in and of itself, so basic, so needed for creativity and innovation, has never been a subject of study. Studying, explaining, and classifying newness led me to the creation of a new science—Novology, the science of newness (for more information, see my article "Novology, the Science of Newness, for Creativity and Innovation Research" in *The Future of Creativity*, Scholastic Testing Services, 2002).

If you want to be a genius, learn how to spot the type of newness that will bring about millions of changes. Go for a million. That is the Third Law of MegaCreativity.

By this law, I mean that a MegaCreator focuses on generating ideas so fundamental that in turn they generate other ideas. A MegaCreator is an innovator, bringing ideas to society where they will inspire other ideas. In this way, a MegaCreator can become a MegaInnovator and change the world.

Chapter Eight

MegaInnovate

Genius does what it must, and Talent does what it can.

OWEN MEREDITH

This chapter will show you how a new vision of innovation can change how you view your own mind. Now that your mind is capable of nonlinear creative thinking that leads to a million new ideas per minute, and now that you know how to find the essential newness that will lead to millions of changes, maybe it is time to call it the MegaInnovative mind. Our task is to find out how to transfer as many ideas to society as society accepts, and much more (for future societies).

GROWING YOUR MEGAINNOVATIVE MIND

This task and increasing our creativity require a free and open mind, one that is trained to find solutions quickly. Let's train our brains to think more quickly, to spot the answer despite distractions from meaningless information. To do that, try the puzzles that follow. You will recognize some of the puzzles, but you may have forgotten the answers. Some puzzles will be new to you. You might ask your children to help you. Have fun and enjoy the ride!

Sample Puzzle
Imagine you are the driver of a truck. In the morning, you have to load the truck with three boxes of apples and five

boxes of oranges. In the afternoon, you also load six boxes of watermelons and five boxes of plums. How old is the driver? I know you may be puzzled. Nevertheless, the problem stands. How old is the driver?

The first answer traditionally is: "He must be at least sixteen to have a license."

The second popular answer is: "Nineteen."

I ask, "Why?"

"Well . . . 3 + 5 + 6 + 5 makes 19."

I shake my head.

Soon my students ask me to repeat the problem. I am happy to hear their request. The rule in my classes stays the same, "If you do not have something, ask!" (If students ask, they show they are active. Teachers love it.)

Since you are reading this book, you can go back to the problem and read it again.

Got it? Got the answer?

Not yet?

When my students ask me to repeat it for the second time, I change the number of boxes and I add other fruits and vegetables to confuse them more. They still think that the age of a driver is somehow connected with these numbers of boxes. The age of the driver will not change if there are twelve, thirty-four, or seventy-six boxes. The age of the driver has nothing to do with the boxes. Read the puzzle again, and exclude all the information about the boxes. Read the first sentence and the last sentence.

Got it?

Good! What is the age of the driver? Write it here: _____

If you wrote your age, you're right. The solution is simple. *You* are the driver of the truck. How old are *you*?

Here is the explanation. Math often turns off our thinking and turns on calculation. When the brain sees or hears figures and numbers, it automatically begins to count. We've been conditioned by math classes.

In reality, mathematics must be predetermined by mathsemantics (for more information, see a wonderful book by Edward MacNeal, *Mathsemantics: Making Numbers Talk Sense*, Viking Penguin Books, 1994). Semantics is the science of meaning, of understanding the meaning, so Mathsemantics insists: understanding first, calculations later. Somebody smart said that math is like a grinder: Put meat there, and you get meat, but if you put grass there, expect to get grass.

The problem with the driver puzzle is typical of the so-called method of excessive information (MEI). It gives you a lot of information that is not needed for the solution. Moreover, this information diverts your thinking from the solution.

There is a theory I am fond of that says there are about forty *types* of problems. If you learn how to solve all forty types of problems, then you will be able to easily solve all the problems in your life. If you miss some types, you will have problems unsolved.

If we teach all children these forty types of problems, imagine how fast they would be and how successful they would be!

To see that the driver puzzle is really a type of problem, try the next puzzle.

Puzzle 1

Imagine that you are the driver of a trolley. On the first stop six people come in, on the second stop three come out and five come in, and on the third stop two passengers come out and seven come in. What is the age of the driver? (I like this version, too: What color are the driver's eyes?)

Puzzle 2

How many fingers do you see in this picture?

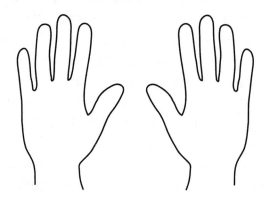

So, how many fingers will be there on ten hands? Write it fast: _____

Solve all the puzzles, and then check the answers starting on page 90.

Puzzle 3

A police officer chases a criminal from the first to the fifth floor. How many flights of stairs will the police officer cover?

The police officer did not get the criminal and has to run from the fifth to the tenth floor. How many flights of stairs does he have to cover on the way from the fifth to the tenth floor?

Puzzle 4

Five crows are sitting on a tree. Three of them are about to fly away. How many of the crows are left on the tree?

Puzzle 5

How many animals of every species did Moses take onto the ark?

Puzzle 6

One slope of a roof is sixty degrees, and another slope is thirty degrees. A rooster laid an egg on top of the roof. Which way will the egg fall?

Puzzle 7

A snail crawls around a stadium. When it crawls clockwise, it finishes the circle in an hour and a half. When it crawls counterclockwise, it covers the circle in ninety minutes. Why is there a difference?

Puzzle 8

This is a law question. An airplane flying from Dallas to Mexico crashed on the border. Where will they bury the survivors?

Puzzle 9

Here is a figure made of some matches:

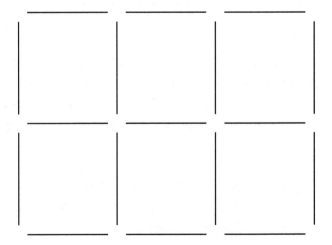

1. Take away three matches to leave four squares (boxes). When solved, put all the matches back.
2. Now, take away four matches to leave only three squares (boxes).

Puzzle 10

I give you two coins that total thirty cents, but one of them is not a quarter. How?

ANSWERS

Puzzle 1

The trolley driver is your age because the first sentence states, "Imagine that you are the driver of a trolley." (Another version is, "The eyes are mine, so they are. . . .")

Puzzle 2

Fifty. There are only five fingers on one hand, so ten hands will make fifty, not one hundred as you probably answered. What you see is two hands (not one). So the calculation must be different: two hands = ten fingers. Ten hands are five times more than two: $10 \times 5 = 50$.

Puzzle 3

In the first case, four flights of stairs (you don't count the first floor because you stand on it: $5 - 1 = 4$). In the second case, five flights of stairs ($10 - 5 = 5$). Check it with a drawing. Usually, the mind is tricked into saying, "The same."

Puzzle 4

All of the crows because they are only "*about* to fly," not already flew away (if you counted $5 - 3 = 2$, then math is turning off your thinking again).

Puzzle 5

None. It was Noah, not Moses (again the question "how many" turns off your thinking).

Puzzle 6

None. Roosters don't lay eggs. If you tried to solve the problem by comparing the numbers, you are again taken away by the numbers.

Puzzle 7

There is no difference: an hour and a half = ninety minutes.

Puzzle 8

Survivors are not buried—they are survivors. You were distracted by the words *legal* and *bury*.

Puzzle 9

1. Take out three central horizontal matches, and the remaining matches will make four separated boxes (your mind assumes that somehow they must be connected).
2. Take away the cross section (four matches from the inside), and the rest will make one big box and two little ones (your mind incorrectly assumes that they must be equal).

Puzzle 10

A nickel and a quarter. Remember, one of them (the nickel) is not a quarter. You are deceived by the phrase "one of them is not."

TRAINING YOUR INNOVATIVE ABILITIES

Now that your brain is sharp from these fun puzzles, let's move to some real problems that will help us innovate and thereby Go for a Million. A trained brain is the same as a trained body—it reacts better, it works better, and it stays alert longer.

In the previous chapter, we found that the main feature of innovation is the transfer of newness from the individual to a social group. Having found this new, simple solution for the essence of innovation, we now have to apply this vision to our new reality to improve it. For us to do it better, we need to learn some general things that will save us from confusion.

Novology, the science of newness, holds that there are five universal levels available in anything: in nature, the universe, life, history, education, etc. These levels are:

- **Existential**: Everything must *exist* or come into *existence* before anything happens to it.
- **Relational**: When something exists, it *relates* to or communicates with all other existing things and processes. Also called communicational.
- **Instrumental**: Out of all relations established on the relational level, *instrumental* ones are of the most importance, and they lead to the creation of *instruments* or tools.
- **Orientational**: These instruments and tools have to be properly *oriented* to the benefit of the outer world (the environment, society, social values).
- **Innovational**: Everything transferred (given to and accepted by) the society is an *innovation* that brings new objects, new features, new pro-

cesses into existence. The cycle then starts again and goes to the first (existential) level.

Novology holds that these five levels repeat themselves in every successful enterprise, in every successful event—even in a successful school lesson. Our analysis also showed that geniuses somehow (intuitively or not) follow these five levels, and that is why they are successful. In this book you will further understand these levels, and you'll learn how to use them to increase your success.

Novology also involves a classification of newness, and the most important classes of newness, taken from philosophy, are the classes of ideal and material newness. Ideal newness is intangible, invisible, untouchable, unobservable by others, etc. It involves reflections, images, ideas, impressions, and meanings. Material newness is tangible, visible, touchable, observable by others, etc. It involves things, objects, and processes.

We move through these two types of newness constantly. We reflect on situations, we think, we create new material objects, things, and processes, and we reflect on them over and over again.

The more ideas and the better ideas you have, the higher is the probability of your success.

Now you can apply this vision to the analysis of your reality and the innovations you are working on.

Existential Innovations
(Innovations on the Level of Existence)
- making (and even to some extent acquiring) new clothes, silverware, appliances, lamps, etc.

- planting new trees and flowers in the yard
- fixing the house
- building (buying, bringing) new furniture for the home
- and so on—new things brought to your existence and changing your existence

People build (buy, trade, plant, paint, fix) things to make their homes, offices—their existence—different. They innovate on the existential level. Though many don't perceive this as innovation, it is.

Communicational Innovations
(Everything New in the Sphere of Communications)

- pronouncing phrases and new expressions in communication
- trying new intonations
- using new words
- practicing new forms of communication (like sign language)
- using and inventing new slang
- offering new languages (like Esperanto, invented by L.L. Zamenhof)

People speak—compose and pronounce words and phrases that solve current problems—on all levels of social life. They wrap up the newness of their individual perceptions, thoughts, feelings, and conclusions into the newness of their phrases and sentences. They deliver this newness to other people through communication channels (voice, phone, radio, TV), and other people consume this newness, evaluate it, and react on this basis. Our society literally changes with every communication act. Sometimes, it's a small change, but it's a change nevertheless. Sometimes it's a big change (like war or revolution), and the reason for it may be one wrong word, one offensive phrase, one awkward text. Authors Peter and Mary Funk, in *Word Power Made Simple,* even state that the nuclear bomb was dropped on Hiroshima because the translator misinterpreted the words of the emperor. Communicational newness is as important as any other type of newness and innovation.

If I could use a math formula, I would call this level "innovation $\times$ innovation = innovation squared = innovation^2." "Squared" in this case means that matter innovation (substance, matter, things) is reflected by words (symbols, signs); thus, there are now two layers. It is less solid than material objects; it is relational and relative, but it is a layer. (For more information on creative linguistics, see my article "Sozidolinguistics for Creative Behavior," *The Journal of Creative Behavior,* 28/2, 1994.)

The word or phrase is the result of creativity, but actually using it in communication is already innovation (the size of the innovation is another issue).

Instrumental Innovations

- offering and accepting new tools (new shovel, new computer, new car, new cell phone)
- offering new methods, techniques, and rules of actions

People produce (invent and build) new tools, and then they sell them to other people. Individuals and society need new tools for getting new results: a new computer for faster document production, a new telephone for better communication, a new car for more reliable transportation, a new iron for easier ironing, a new toothbrush for better cleaning. Tools offered and accepted (consummated) are like selling "third-power" innovations—tools are new by themselves, but they also bring some innovative results.

If I could use a math formula, I would call this level "innovation $\times$ innovation $\times$ innovation = innovation cubed = innovation^3." "Cubed" in this case means that the instrumental layer is over the communicational layer—it is material again; it is tangible, observable, touchable. It is the innovation of transferring new tools and instruments to people.

Orientational Innovations
(Social Problem Solving)

- teaching the skills to apply tools in a certain situation
- providing the sense of social orientation to any instrument, knowledge, or data

People intentionally or unintentionally discover new ways to do things. Instruments are important, but the situations they're used in, the problems they solve, the skills they require, the manners of using them for variants of the problem, must be acquired from society. Teaching, training, coaching, and so on are ways to transfer this experience of orientation. These processes are transferring the orientational newness, and people who produce new methods and techniques to solve problems faster are in the business of orientational innovation. When they show these methods and techniques to other people through personal example, classes, workshops, books, TV shows, and so on, other people learn (consume this newness) and become more experienced. Society becomes smarter.

If I could use a math formula, I would call this level "innovation $\times$ innovation $\times$ innovation $\times$ innovation = innovation (fourth power) = innovation^4." "Fourth power" in this case means that matter innovation (substance, matter, things) is again reflected by words (symbols, signs), descriptions, images, schemes, and by describing situations, tools, and actions. Now it is ideal again, it is relational and relative, but it is also more complex. It is social problem–oriented. It must take into account people, their needs, their troubles, etc.

Innovational Innovations
- reporting (new physical phenomena, i.e., in science)
- patenting (new technical decisions, i.e., in technology)
- publishing (articles, books, magazines, journals, Internet)
- broadcasting (radio, TV)
- producing art shows (new pictures, sculptures, etc.)
- performing (at the theater, movies, concerts)

To a large extent, people of this level are newness-oriented. They are thirsty for newness production and newness transfer. They think of new articles, new books, new performances, new exhibitions, and new TV shows, and they make them happen. In this field, producing and transferring newness becomes so obvious that it is even called *news*: *news*papers, technological *news*, political *news*, evening *news*. Inventors, scientists, authors, actors, and reporters are in the field of discoveries, inventions, copyrights, designs, and so on. All types of intellectual property protected by laws are involved here. This is the level of professional innovators—newness producers and newness transferrers.

If I could use a math formula, I would call this level "innovation $\times$ innovation $\times$ innovation $\times$ innovation $\times$ innovation = innovation (fifth power) = innovation^5." "Fifth power" in this case means that innovation is again reflected and offered in the form of news reporting (patents, articles, books, shows, performances)—each form reports the news to the broadest public.

As a rule, this fifth layer is universally accepted as the innovation layer. The orientational layer is less often seen as innovational, and the instrumental layer is very seldom seen as innovational.

For example, Alexander Graham Bell, the inventor of the telephone, is well known and is in the history books. However, the telephone "improver"—even if the person made the leap to a cellular version—is not known, despite the fact that the tool is very different. In this case, a telephone remains a telephone, and nobody cares how it works—through wires or without them. It is looked upon as the same or nearly the same instrument. The addition of the word *cellular* may sell more, but it will not make the inventor a genius in the public eye. Alexander Graham Bell will still hold the title.

The communicational layer is seen as even less innovational, but new things are exploding in this layer. New words, new phrases, and new expressions are invented and used in every minute of communication. They bring smiles, they are remembered and repeated, but they are very seldom viewed as innovations. Exceptions to the rule are words that can be traced to their first use in the written language. Then, when the word appears in the dictionary, it can be traced to the year and sometimes the author. For example, Marie Curie, who worked with materials that radiated X rays invisible to human eyes, coined the word *radioactive.*

Finally, the existential layer is not viewed as innovational at all, until a change of existential environment is viewed as fashion and is made into a model home or a magazine or journal subject. Otherwise, only you as an owner, your friends, your neighbors know about the new things you acquire.

CLIMBING TO THE GENIUS LEVEL

With such layers, it is easy to see the high-layer innovation and the low-layer innovation. Interestingly, even the lowest-layer innovation has a chance to leap to the high layer. On the other hand, even the highest-layer innovation can lose its edge and slip down. Thus, innovation as a process goes on and on and on. Now that you have been introduced to the layers of innovation, you can choose which layer to exploit, which layer is your next step.

For example, let's say you are good at improving your house—you love making your existence easier and more pleasant. Let's see how knowing the layers of innovation can help you climb to the genius level.

1. **Existential layer**. Existentially, you are successful.

2. **Communicational layer**. You invite guests to your house, and they are amazed and surprised. They *ask* you how you did it, and you *tell* them. The community begins to *talk* about you as a talented designer. Obviously, this is the second layer—the layer of communication.

3. **Instrumental layer**. You explain the different tools you used (concepts, instruments, pictures, models) to the specialists who are interested.

4. **Orientational layer**. You help other people improve their environments (solve their problems). Would you become a consultant? A designer?

5. **Innovational level**. News must be transferred to a maximum broad society. Would you like to write an article? A book? Would you like to have a TV show? Some people who teach how to become successful will tell you to write a column for the newspaper, arrange radio interviews, and so on. You now know why! That is the broadest community you can share your nowness with.

Let's take another example: Imagine that you are very good at making up jokes. Maybe rhymes come naturally to your mind. This is certainly communicational newness (new jokes, new poems), but you have to know how to be accepted (not rejected) and how to go to the level of genius. Please analyze your next steps:

1. Existential layer_____

2. Communicational layer_____

3. Instrumental layer_____

4. Orientational layer_____

5. Innovational layer_____

Now, when you practiced the layers of innovation and steps you have to take to climb to the genius level on the other examples, you can do it with your personal strength. Write what your strength is and analyze what your steps will be to become a genius.

1. Existential layer_____

2. Communicational layer_____

3. Instrumental layer_____

4. Orientational layer_____

5. Innovational layer_____

Apply the knowledge. Fill in the blanks. Elaborate every stage. Think of as many activities as possible, and then choose wisely what to do. Then success is guaranteed—no mistakes. All is scientifically based and proven. That is why I say that Novology, the science of newness that I introduced, explains everything and helps innovators of all domains determine the stable routes to success.

CONTINUE TO TRAIN YOUR MIND
Your mind is capable of achieving MegaCreativity. Your mind now knows how to see the essential innovations

that will cause millions of other innovations. However, the mind itself—your MegaInnovative Mind, the mind of a genius—still needs training.

A MegaInnovative Mind is more than just an ability—it is your mind actively employing and implementing Mega-Creativity into your life. If a normal mind offers several improvements in a lifetime, then a MegaInnovative mind offers thousands and millions of improvements. Moreover, if a normal mind offers low quality innovative ideas and consequently lower level newness improvements, then a MegaInnovative mind offers ten-, one hundred-, one thousand-, and one million-fold increases and improvements.

Finally, for those of you undecided, consider this: If innovation is just a transfer of the found newness, and we do it every day (in small or big portions), then why be scared in front of a bigger audience? Why be nervous before the presentation? Why be afraid of public speaking? Teaching innovation must be the task of school, the mission of innovative education. The issue is how to move our innovative power to the level where it will be seen by millions. Famous artists, actors, and scientists do this all the time. Now it is your turn! With the methods you have learned, you can do it. Every one of us has some pictures to show, some inventions or bright ideas to share, or some artistic actions to perform. The question now is, what layer of innovation are we working at, and what is the next step in the spread of your innovation?

Do what you must do, just as geniuses do. Your horizons are much broader and your obligations are much more serious than those of a mere talent. "Genius does what it must, and Talent does what it can."

Chapter Nine

Get Out
of the
System

Away with Systems! Away with a corrupt world! Let
us breathe the air of the Enchanted Island.

GEORGE MEREDITH

Now that you know the differences between creativity and
innovation, you are ready to learn some visually based
structures that will consciously lead you to the highest
possible innovations. To reach that level, you must go
beyond the system of normalized thinking. You must literally follow the popular phrase, *Break out of the box*. This
chapter will show you five necessary steps that every genius has to get through to achieve the best result: to become a mega-recognized MegaInnovator.

Here are some exercises to help you understand how
it can be done.

Connect the four dots below with three straight lines.
Start and finish at the same spot, without picking up your
pen or pencil and without going back.

●　　●

●　　●

If you know the answer, do the exercise and then go to the next task.

If you do not know the answer, find it. It may take some time, but it will be very useful.

If you spend more than ten minutes on this exercise, here is a hint: Get out of the box! The solution is out of the box!

Check whether you found the answer. Your thinking probably followed this pattern:

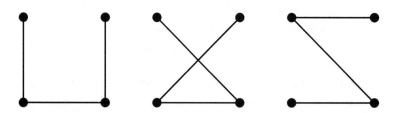

Obviously these forms do not start and finish in the same spot. Have you found the right answer? Some of you may feel that there is no solution, and some of you may be frustrated. This is understandable. The tension is growing.

Let me state it again here: Find the solution. It is beyond the box limits!

If you move on without solving the problem, you will gain knowledge of how to do it, but it will not develop your creative thinking. Geniuses never knew the solution. They thought it over and over again, until it clicked: "Aha!" I urge you to try to do it yourself.

When you think you have found the solution, continue reading.

Some of the most creative (though not right yet) decisions are like this:

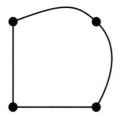

It certainly is more creative than the previous solutions, but this is not a straight line.

If your decision was like that, you're partially on the right track. At least you are out of the system—or out of the box.

Try some other versions. I repeat: three straight lines, starting and finishing at the same spot without going back and without picking up your hand.

I see some of you making it like this:

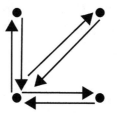

This is starting and finishing at the same spot, but you are still going back. Nice try, though!

Once you think you found the solution, continue reading.

Here is the correct solution:

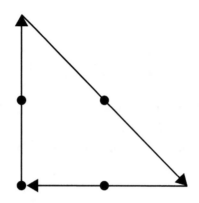

If your solution was correct, my question is, "Did you try to find one more solution, or did you just turn the page?"

Do you remember the First Law of MegaCreativity? Quit Quitting! It means: Go ahead, do more than you are asked to do. When you find a second solution, continue reading.

TURN THE PAGE
FOR THE
NEXT SOLUTION

Here is the second solution:

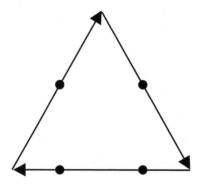

Now you see that there are solutions. If you were frustrated, then it was only your personal reaction. Nature has these solutions, but our minds are not yet strong enough to find them. Here is where the training comes in handy. It trains us not to get frustrated, to have fun, and still find the solutions.

Creativity is fun. It is more fun than anything else. When you create your own solution, you get a wonderful feeling of satisfaction: Ahh!

However, let's go back to our problem.

I used this problem here on purpose. I wanted to show you that when your mind sees a box (four dots forming a box), it tends to stay in the box. It takes a special effort to get out of the box, or out of the system. *A truly creative solution is always out of the system.* Every system, just because it is a system, is a limitation. A creative mind must look first for solutions out of the system.

Michael Kirton, the author of *Kirton Adaptor/Innovator Inventory (KAI)* uses the term *innovator* to describe people who tend to change the system instead of adapting it. From his point of view, it is just another style of creativity to be an innovator.

In general, I disagree with Kirton's point of view. I also disagree with his usage of terminology (*adaptor* vs. *innovator*), but in this particular case our points of view come closer. Getting out of the system (or changing the system of reference) *is* more innovative, or in correct terms, more new, than to stay within the system.

Now let's go back to the problem solutions. I want to show you visually how your mind had to get out of the system to solve the problem. Here's where it happened:

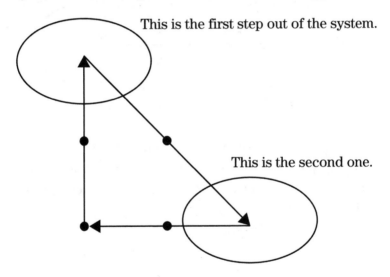

This is the first step out of the system.

This is the second one.

In the second solution there were three cases when your mind had to get out of the box:

This is the first one.

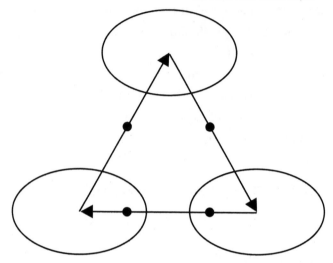

This is the third one.   This is the second one.

So actually, these are two different solutions. Have you enjoyed them? Are you ready for another problem? Say, "Yes!" Say it loud! Say it louder! Put some energy into it because it will be really tough!

Here is another problem:

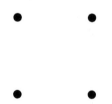

Cross these four dots with two straight parallel lines crossing each other.

Some of my students at once say, "Parallel? They never cross. . . ."

Well, let me restate it for you to be sure this is not a word trick: The task is to cross these four dots with *two straight parallel lines crossing each other.*

Try it.

If you can find a solution, I personally would consider that you have a genius mind—a mind with a genius potential. If you spend more than twenty minutes and the solution is not there, turn to the next page.

When my students give up, which happens often on this problem, I say, "Okay, when the problem is unsolvable or looks unsolvable, a normal mind would give up, but a genius mind would go for a tougher problem. A more difficult problem may throw some light on an easier one."

Check yourself now. Which would you prefer? Give up (quit) or keep trying (quit quitting) and have a more difficult problem?

If you give up, you can find the solution on a page that you have to calculate:

Have a number in your head.

Add the same number to it.

Divide it by the first number.

Multiply it by six.

Add 101 to it, and you can go to this page.

If you prefer the genius way—the more difficult way—continue with the next problem:

● ●

● ●

You might smile or shrug your shoulders in irritation when you see these four dots again. However, life is life. In the majority of life situations, we are not choosing the problems. They come by themselves. However, every one of your solutions teaches you how to solve problems.

This problem is tougher than the first two. You have to cross these four dots with one straight line. Let me repeat it: One line must go through these four dots, and it must be straight.

Some people ask, "How thick can I make the line?"

Right! That's the solution: It's a thick line. It is a simple (genius type) solution.

Let me explain the psychological barrier that was in your head. Since childhood, since school, since geometry class, everybody knows that a line has only one dimension—length. Right? This becomes such a block in your mind that you don't remember that lines may be thin and thick. There are thin and thick brushes, thin and thick pens, thin and thick lines on your computer. A line of people waiting for something is called a line. I bet it is not thin. A line of cars is even thicker. They are still lines. What about the lines dividing the road? They are thick, too.

Some of you might say: "Gosh, that was stupid!" Maybe you're right, but this is the reality of the mind—this is how it works. It is full of limitations, and these limitations do look stupid when you overcome them.

Now, having solved this task (of higher difficulty), could you go back and solve the second problem? Cross four dots with two straight parallel lines!

Got it? Yes, now it is obvious! There are at least two solutions.

SOLUTION 1 (GRAPHIC SOLUTION)

The lines are thick and they are partially overlaid on one another. Thus, they "cross" over each other, they have a cross section, and they are still parallel.

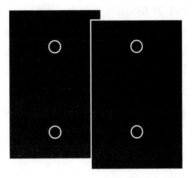

SOLUTION 2 (MATHEMATICAL SOLUTION)

Our "knowledge" that "parallel lines never cross" comes from when we studied geometry in school. Not many of us remember that the teacher said it was Euclid who first offered this geometry. We rarely remember that the teacher said it was geometry of flat surfaces and that there were five postulates—laws accepted without proof. The postulate of parallel lines was one of them. No proof. You have to believe it if you want some other regularities to work. (By the way, a few other postulates were "dots have no dimensions," and "a line, consisting of dots, has only one dimension—length.")

So the problems stated previously actually challenged two of the postulates. You have already seen that lines have width and length. Thus, we got rid of one limitation. Some mathematicians—long before us—challenged the postulate of the parallel lines, too, and they came to strange results. Russian mathematician Nikolai Lobachevski and American mathematician Bernhard Riemann discovered it nearly simultaneously, and it led to a new geometry: Non-Euclidean Geometry. It is also called the geometry of curved spaces (non-flat!) because flat surfaces turned out to be just a particular case. Therefore, Euclidean geometry is just a particular case in the generic geometry. But our mind accepts it as if the geometry teacher were God, and everything that she said was true forever. This is where we were taught *not* to get out of the system, where we learned to think with minimum creativity.

So here it is:

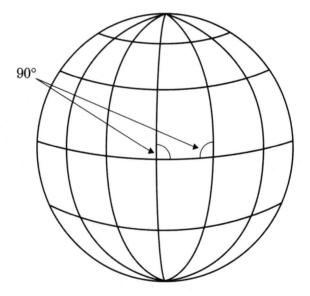

Meridians (vertical lines) cross the equator (horizontal central line), and the angle between any meridian and the equator is ninety degrees. So, according to Euclid, they are parallel, but all meridians cross at the poles. Imagine that our four dots are placed near the equator and they are crossed by two meridians. These meridians are parallel and they also cross!

This geometry may seem strange, but it is correct. In fact, it is used for space flight calculations. Why? Because the space around the Earth, and the Earth itself, is not flat. A flat surface (plane) is only a particular case that was easier to research, find regularities on, and describe. That's why Euclid did it first more than two thousand years ago. It took humanity that long to overcome the mental barrier and develop another geometry.

There are other solutions besides the graphic and mathematical solutions. If you can find one or two more, send them to me.

Look at it this way: Euclidean geometry (when taught to everybody at school) becomes a box.

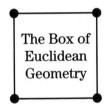

The Box of Euclidean Geometry

Your task is to get out of the box. By saying, "Hey, this is only one type of geometry. Maybe there are other types," you are out of the box. Or another version: "Hey, this is geometry, but life is more than geometry." Just like that, you're free. Find some "lines" that are different from geometrical lines and solve the problem.

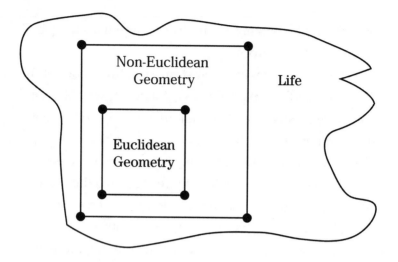

Again, the conclusion is simple. Here are the five steps to a better (maybe even genius) solution:

1. Believe that the solutions are available. (They exist.)
2. Remember that the solutions are out of the system (related to some other supersystem).
3. Define the given system. (What is a line? What is parallel? Which geometry?) Definitions are instruments, but they *de-fine*, or make things finite—limited. Use them to "unlimit" yourself. Name another system or super system that includes the given system.
4. Get out of the system (give the line two dimensions instead of one; accept that not all surfaces are flat), and find a new solution.
5. Report your new "out-of-the-system solution" and become a genius, like Lobachevski and Riemann. Or, train your mind to do it like the geniuses did in their time, and look for another huge problem to solve!

How New Is Your New?

If you have solved all the given problems by yourself and you proved that you have a genius mind, you may regret that these problems are just for training. This is understandable. You see the target, you aim for it, you hit the target, and then you see that it's a training target; it has been hit by many people—or by at least one person—long before you. The next skill, therefore, is to learn how to find your own problems—the real ones. The path is also not easy.

Once, as a young Ph.D. candidate working on language problems, I discovered a unit (like Mendel's unit that ended up being called a gene). I woke up in the middle of the night, got up, wrote down everything, and in a week happily reported everything to my scientific mentor, Maryam S. Karayeva. She listened attentively and praised me for deep thinking. Several months later, while reading one of the old works of my mentor, I found a description of a unit in the same layer of the language, named a little bit differently, but having the same essence. The difference in the name that I gave to it was only one letter! Can you imagine my embarrassment? What would my teacher think of me? I called my mentor, asked for a meeting, came to talk, reminded her of our previous talk, and, blushing, apologized. She calmed me down and said she saw it had not been plagiarism. She also added, "It showed to me that you were heading in the right direction." That was a relief and a big lesson—both scientific and humane. You must know that I loved my mentor. She was, is, and will always be, my example to follow.

So as you see, we rediscover things and find that some

of what we thought was new could have existed for a long time. This is called *subjectively new* vs. *objectively new*. Subjectively new is something new to a person (to a subject), and objectively new is something new to all people. I personally dislike these terms because they don't contrast subject and object. They assume that one person has a subjective (biased, "not right") opinion, while a group of people has an objective (unbiased, "right") opinion. A subjective opinion of an individual may be right or wrong, but the seemingly "objective" opinion of all people may be right or wrong, too. For example, all people thought the Earth was flat until Magellan proved it was a ball.

So while speaking about newness, I prefer to say *individually new, family new, neighborhood new, city new, country new, world new,* or just *socially new*. Precise terminology eliminates mistakes. It also becomes clear that the rank of newness needs probing, testing, reporting, and comparing—this is all innovative activity. This innovative activity is complex, dangerous, and sometimes unpleasant, but it is absolutely necessary.

Imagine if after the fiasco with my "new unit" I had decided to quit. I would have never discovered other units, other laws, and other sciences. Imagine also that somebody in your family is negative—your new ideas may be stomped at once, and if you do not have courage, you will never show them to the bigger society. Dr. E. Paul Torrance likes to say that creativity requires courage: The moment you generate a new idea you are the minority of one. However, before you solve a problem you have to find one. Let me also state that not only the solution to the problem, but even stating the problem, can be very creative. Why would Einstein think of relativity? Why would Louis Pasteur think of bacteria? Why would Madam Curie think of another chemical element?

So you might have seen the first problem with four dots and three lines. However, you have never seen the problem with four dots and two lines or the problem with four dots and one line. Right? I invented them for you. Now you can invent your own problems for me, for your friends, and for others.

Remember, problem stating is as important as problem solving. Learn how to state problems. Learn how to ask questions. Train your curiosity. Train your thinking.

FROM TRADITIONAL THINKING TO INNOVATIVE THINKING

Usually, people contrast creative and critical thinking with just thinking.

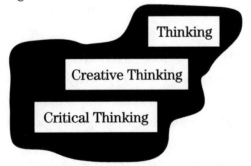

Instead, you should go out of the box and take thinking as a whole—as associative brain activity—and put it into another, bigger triangle. Then I would probably make a picture differentiating all levels of thinking like in the following model:

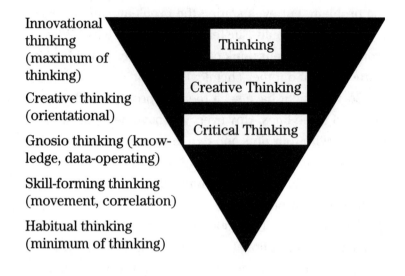

Innovational thinking (maximum of thinking)

Creative thinking (orientational)

Gnosio thinking (knowledge, data-operating)

Skill-forming thinking (movement, correlation)

Habitual thinking (minimum of thinking)

The new model would include all types of thinking in accordance with the five levels but would show the increase in intensity of thinking, in breadth of thinking, and in orientation of thinking from minimum to maximum. This model may be closer to reality than the previous model.

FROM INNOVATIVE THINKING TO MEGAINNOVATIVE THINKING

The next step we have to make here is to move from innovative to highly innovative, or MegaInnovative thinking. This is the type of thinking where one innovation brings millions of changes, or one transfer leads to millions of transfers, such as with the wheel, telephone, telegraph, and computer. A scientific discovery that leads to thousands of inventions and to millions of new products is this type of innovation. This is the newness of highest quality.

Do not confuse the quality of newness with the quality

of a thing or an object. Newness itself can be of low quality and of high quality. For example, a person produces an idea that seems new to her. However, when she presents this idea to others or checks it against the bulk of one's other ideas, it turns out to be a known idea, or an idea close to the ideas already dreamed up.

In my case of offering a new unit, the idea was of low newness, or of low quality newness. Newness quality depends on a comparison, and it must breach at least five easily identifiable contours to be considered a high quality newness: individual, family, direct neighborhood (enterprise, school), direct geo-vicinity (city, country), and global.

A potential invention, for example, must be a globally new, technical idea. To qualify for a patent, one of fifteen thousand researchers working for the U.S. Patent and Trademark Office checks the idea against all existing technical patents and must find it to be new. So a patent holder, at the moment of getting the patent, is placed onto the top of the newness hierarchy. The feeling, I have to tell you, is invigorating. My son, my wife, and I experienced it in 1984 when our technical work was certified as an invention, and we received "the red corner." (In Russia, the Certificate of Invention had a red corner on it and actually was used as a patent level document.)

The same statement about the newness hierarchy can be applied to a discovery. A discovery, as the highest possible newness, is compared to all possible sources, and if found unique, makes the person a discoverer. Discovery is finding a new object, phenomenon, or regularity existing in nature. It adds nothing to nature—it just makes the human vision different. Nevertheless, discovery leads to numerous inventions (new technical ideas), new actions (as in the discovery of America), and new opportunities. Discovery is higher in the rank of newness than invention because discovery deals with new reality in the material world. When discovered, as in the case of electromagnetism (Michael Faraday), this one discovery can lead to thousands of inventions. What do you think is more important? What do you think is of higher rank?

A discovery may lead to billions of consequences (changes). Certainly it may be considered a GigaInnovation. Discoverers have an excellent chance of staying in the history of humanity, in the books, in the school programs, and in the millions of millions of further transfers.

Transferring the found newness is nice, but transferring it to millions of people or users is certainly nicer. Consider this while thinking of the innovation you are going to make.

In addition to scientific or technical, it may be an educational MegaInnovation—when one transfer (a super-teacher) explains it to thousands of other teachers, and these teachers transfer it to millions of students. It may also be artistic transfer, when one picture or one sculpture is transferred to the publisher and this publisher makes millions of copies of books, tapes, sculptures, movies, and so on. When sold or given away, the items constitute transfer of newness again. It is less valuable newness because it is a copy, but it is still a transfer.

A human mind engaged in the activity of transferring newness on this level of intensity must be considered a MegaInnovative mind. This is the mind of a genius!

So before you say a word, inhale. Think: How new is your statement? How good is it for the people around you? How needed is it? Before you say something for the camera, for the TV or radio show, hold your breath and ask yourself if your words have a quality newness that will resonate with millions. Will you be remembered for this? Inhale and think deeply before you say a word. Then shout loudly, "Away with systems! Let us breathe the air of the Enchanted Island!"

MegaValue People

Being unwanted, unloved, uncared for, forgotten by
everybody, I think that is a much greater hunger, a
much greater poverty than the person who has
nothing to eat . . .

We must find each other.

MOTHER TERESA

Since you learned that to become a genius you have to be
MegaCreative and MegaInnovative, then the task now is
obvious. Learn how to create outstanding solutions for
people's problems. Learn how to internalize and learn to
use the most powerful methods of increasing creativity.
Make them your second nature. This is the step over the
horizon, over the limits of usual and traditional thinking.
In this step you will learn and practice methods and techniques that will automatically send you over the traditional mind limitations.

This section will train your mind on the basis of educational and real problems. Such training will enable you to
orient your knowledge for the socially needed areas, for
the social problems.

Chapter Ten

From Single Perception to MegaImagination

Every creative act

involves . . . a new

innocence of perception,

liberated from the

cataract of accepted

belief.

ARTHUR KOESTLER

This chapter will help you understand that creativity starts at the level of perception and makes its way up to the level of top intellectual functions.

How many squares do you see in this picture?

At once, you probably will say sixteen . . . then seventeen.

Can you see more?

If you look longer, you will see twenty-one . . . twenty-two.

Then twenty-six . . . then thirty . . . then. . . .

It takes some time, but finally you will say, "Many more."

That's right! Many, many more.

How about sixty? One student's solution was, "There are black squares (lines) and white squares (within lines)." So, everything we found before just doubled.

One solution is that the picture is a cube, and we see only one side of it—we can't see all the other squares.

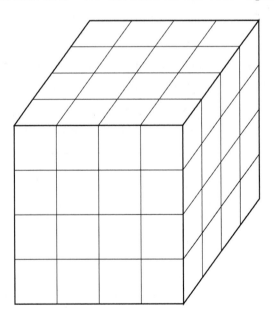

A pretty neat solution is "infinite number"; this may be the Great Wall of China seen from the side—it goes thousands of miles, but we don't see all the cubes and squares now. There may be millions of squares inside of the cube.

Good! No matter how many squares you managed to find, it is more than when you started. Your mind went from sixteen to infinity in just a few minutes.

What is most interesting is that the picture itself never changed. It was and is the same picture. What really changed was your perception. Certainly, it takes time to "see" something new in the same picture, so when you give yourself time, the magic happens: You begin to "see" what you have never seen. You create another vision.

WORKING ON YOUR MEGAIMAGINATION

Thus, your creativity starts from the level of perception. You are the creator of your images, your visions, and your fantasies.

Several people can look at the same cloud, and one might see it as a cloud, one might see it as a sheep, one might see it as a clown, and so on. Take your time. Create your own vision. Create your ability to create new images. Furthermore, create yourself as a creator of these visions.

Artists just grab pencils and begin to sketch these pictures, writers describe them in their works, actors show them in their performances, and businesspeople see them in their dreams—all are creative and all create. Train your brain to never stop at one image. Train your brain to quit quitting, and learn to go for a million, or even to infinity, to the point beyond the horizon. Then, your mind will be ready to create genius solutions, and it will often do it automatically.

Literature on creativity includes a number of exercises that you can use to work on your perception.

Sid Parnes, for instance, gives a useful exercise in his book *Optimizing the Magic of Your Mind.* He asks his readers, "If I tell you that four makes half of eight, will you agree?" People say, "Yes." Then he says, "If I tell you that zero makes half of eight, will you agree?" After some thinking, nearly all agree, too (though it takes some time to grasp that the figure "8" consists of two zeroes standing on each other). Then he says, "If I tell you that three makes half of eight, will you agree?" Now everybody sees that a vertical cut of eight will make two threes. Then he goes to two, five, six, and even one. Try it yourself.

What is important from my point of view is the connection of perception with mental reflection, known as *categorizing.* This involves not only envisioning something, but also naming it. Here is how I teach this in my classes:

I ask my students to explain what they see.

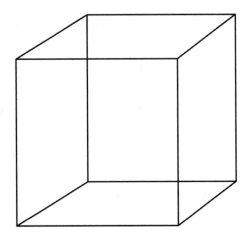

A cube.

Do you see it from below or from above?
Both.

Let me tell you that you see *both*, but not together. You see either this or that. Your mind makes a leap from one vision to another.

Look at the next picture. Give yourself a chance to see both the images, and you will feel a kind of "Aha!" As Sid Parnes says, this can be a five-volt, a ten-volt, or even a one thousand-volt "Aha!"

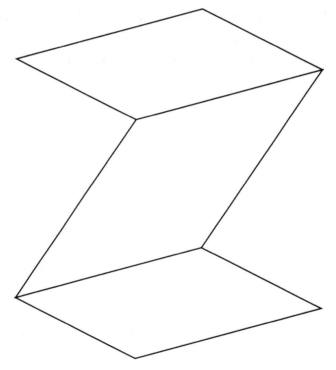

Do you see how it turns from side to side? Good.

Look at the next picture. Does it go from left to right, or from right to left?

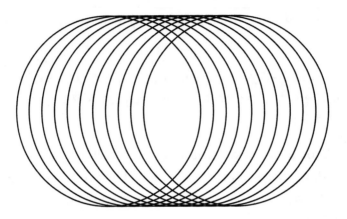

Take a look at this picture. Do you see it as a staircase or a decoration hanging from the ceiling?

If you see both, then look at the next picture.

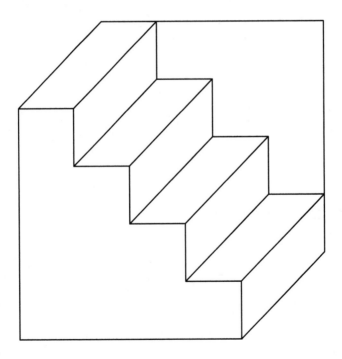

Do you see the plane going away from you or coming toward you? Look at it until you see both images.

I'm sure you will like this next picture. What do you see first: a duck or a rabbit? When you can see both in turn, go to the next picture.

What do you see first: the face of a woman or a saxophone player?

Once you see one image, train yourself to change the image in your mind. Do it several times.

The next picture will be very difficult.
What do you see?

This exercise, which proves the most difficult for
some people, produced a one thousand-volt "Aha!" in my
classes. When you see it, there will be no doubt that you
solved the problem.

(Hint: You may rotate the page or turn it from side to
side.)

Be sure it is not a map, or room plan, or an abstract
picture. There is sense in this picture. Take your time if

you don't see it. If you see it or know it, please move on to the next exercise.

Now that you've trained your perception or visioning, I want you to grow even more. Please find the switch from one category to another in every one of the previous pictures.

For example, what are the two opposing categories in the picture of the cube?

Top vs. bottom.

Very good! What are the two opposing categories in the picture of the plane?

To us/away from us.

Right! Now you try: What are the two opposing categories in the picture of the spiral?

_____ *(Say it aloud.)*

Perfect. What are the two opposing categories in the picture of the staircase?

_____ *(Say it aloud.)*

Cool. In what category does your brain dwell in the picture of the folded paper?

_____ *(Say it aloud.)*

What is the category of change in the picture of the duck/rabbit?

_____ *(Say it aloud.)*

What is the category of change in the picture of the folded paper face/saxophone player?

_____ *(Say it aloud.)*

What about the last picture, the one with the letters? Why did it take so much time to guess?

White/black?

No.

Dark/light?

No.

Close/far?

You are getting closer. Those who work with computers, and especially with graphics, do it all the time. They put some things on the . . . and bring other things closer to us.

Background/foreground!

Here you are! Good for you. Remember, your ability to perceive background and foreground is not yet trained to the degree that all other categories are trained—for example, up/down, left/right, away/to. That is why it takes so much more time.

I told you earlier that you need to know how to solve about forty types of puzzles to be able to solve all the puzzles in the world. You also learned how to solve problems (puzzles) with excessive information. All the puzzles you solved in this chapter were just another type—spatial. However, if you learn how to change your perception from one category to another, then you learn them all. To help you see how the training of the mind works, let me show you one more picture.

What is it?

SUCCESS

Success!

Exactly! Here you are, fast and correct! Why?
Because our minds already know the trick!

Perfect! Your mind already knows the way to solve the problem, and even the most difficult one has been solved in a second. This is how a trained mind is faster than a nontrained one.

Note: All the other exercises are optional, but you are welcome to solve them.

TRAINING YOUR MEGAIMAGINATION

Here is one more funny exercise that I use in my classes to train the extreme perceptual ability and the MegaImagination of students. It also trains you to see beyond the surface. You can use these exercises for yourself, for your children, or for your students.

What is this? You will probably say, "A rectangle." What else?

A brick.

What else?

A window.

What else? In reality this is the letter *n* seen from the side. Or, by the way, any other letter. For example, *F, E, e, o. . . .* What else?

A figure like 1 *seen from the side.*

What else?

Any figure, including 2, 3, 5, 6, 7, 8, 9, 0 *made three-dimensional and seen from the top.*

What else?

Any object in the box.

What else?

An empty screen of unusual size (vertical).

What else?

An infinite number of things.

Nice answer! Look at *how* and *why* your mind moved from one idea to the other. I asked you the same question: What else? What else? What else? These are the questions you have to ask yourself all the time. This approach will make you a voracious, MegaImaginative thinker—a genius-type thinker.

Here is another exercise.

What is this?

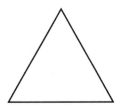

A triangle window to the attic?

Yes, it may be! But for me, it is a figure 3 cut from the paper, folded, and seen from the top.

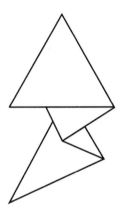

Next question: What is this?

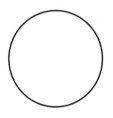

A globe?

What else?
A light on a ship?

What else?
A circle?

What else?
A ball?

Maybe, but for me it is the figure *3* made into the form of a spherical surface and seen from the top. It is like this, but seen from above:

Hmm. Really?

Next question: What is this?

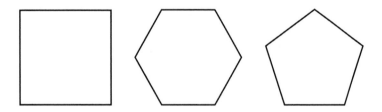

Well, these are probably all figure 3s made in different forms.

How about this one?

You guessed it right! This is a figure 3 exploding. And how about this?

You say it is also the figure 3? I am glad you learned the rules of the game. Everything can be a figure 3. However, this time it is a figure 2 in the mirror (kept at the left side).

Ha-ha!

Sorry to tease you. I meant only to show you that *every* letter and *every* figure can be in millions of shapes, sizes, colors, and materials! Can you imagine the variety of artistic approaches that are possible? Computers make it obvious: hundreds of fonts, sixteen million colors, all forms of shades, etc. There are billions of options.

I know you may be surprised (frustrated? excited? amazed?) by the fact that everything can be everything. Everything *is* everything in the artistic mind—or better to call it the well-developed creative mind. In the highly creative mind there are no blocks. Freedom of association is the best friend of a genius. Genius perception is the ability to see everything in everything! That is why a genius sees the essence where normal people do not.

Now if your perception is more creative and you know what to do to make it a genius perception, we will move to the next chapter, where you will learn more powerful tools to develop your thinking. Some people will call it the relativity of perception, some people will say tastes differ, some people will insist that there is just what they see and nothing else (because of uniqueness of their perceptional history)—this all may be right. My point is different here: You have millions of occasions to see millions of images in every object, whether it is a cloud or a stump. Moreover, you have to train your brain and the brain of your child—and never lose a minute. Instead of aimlessly watching the waves or bodies at the beach, make your mind work—imagine all objects in the same object, create and re-create images. Your MegaCreativity soars with MegaImagination.

Instead of being bored by the dull lecturer, imagine the shadows of his words on the screen behind him.

Instead of idle fidgeting at the airport, enjoy building the muscles of your thinking.

You are the maker of your imagination. You are the creator of your mind. You are the creator of your character because you can be enjoying yourself while others may be frustrated and angry. Your MegaCreativity is your bliss as you work toward greater creative power. Finally, allow other people and other opinions to flourish. Ask what else, what else, what else? Accept their answers and help them grow to MegaImagination, too.

Chapter Eleven

Be Open and MegaOpen

Here is my secret. It's quite simple: One sees clearly
only with the heart. Anything essential is invisible to
the eyes.

ANTOINE DE SAINT-EXUPERY

In previous chapters you learned that even on the level of
physical existence the perception of a more creative person
is different from that of a less creative person. You also
learned special techniques to see the essence with your
mind (chapter six) that you can use to start becoming an
extremely powerful creator—a genius creator. Now it is
time to follow Antoine de Saint-Exupéry's Little Prince and
to learn how to see clearly with your open and MegaOpen
heart.

This chapter will help you get to the next level—the
communicational level—and will teach you skills that will
determine success in further development of your Mega-
Creativity skills. When I say communicational level, I
mean activities that are more than just existence—
activities that include speaking, listening, reading, and
writing. These activities require not only intelligence as it

is usually seen, but creativity as well. In this chapter, you will see the difference between creative and destructive communication. Then, you will learn the steps you can take to move from low-creative (subeffective) communication to high-creative (supereffective) communication.

CREATIVE VS. DESTRUCTIVE COMMUNICATION

In accordance with two main tendencies of nature— creation and destruction—communication can be divided into two types: creative communication and destructive communication.

Creative communication is any communication that creates positive feelings (joy, happiness), understanding (compassion, concern), rapport, desire to work, and—this is very important—the desire to communicate further. Creative communication includes:

- using comfort zones (distances, spaces)
- employing open gestures that show interest (postures)
- attentive (active) listening
- being accepting of information (at least partial, not necessarily complete, agreement)
- supporting idea generation (nonverbal and verbal, including creativity boosters)

Destructive communication is the opposite. It destroys positive feelings and eliminates any desire to communicate further. It shows itself in:

- breaking comfort zones (distances, spaces)
- employing closed, passive, aggressive, or other neg-

ative gestures
- refusing to listen, or using passive/aggressive listening
- negating the information
- throwing "punches" (interruptions, threats, criticism, offensive remarks, creativity squelchers)

Let me state it straightforwardly: On the social level, communication is the starting point for both creation and destruction. It is certainly the starting point of innovation; innovation starts on the social level with the communicative act.

A general rule stemming from the Catastrophe Theory, introduced in 1968 by the French mathematician René Thom, is, "All good is fragile." This means that everything positive is easy to destroy. Usually, "good" is a combination of several contributing positive factors. If one factor in a combination goes wrong, the whole combination ceases to be good. Take, for example, your car. If at least one thing (battery, wheel, brake, or ignition) goes wrong, you are stuck because the car ceases to be "good"—it needs to be fixed.

One of the consequences of the "All good is fragile" law is that creation is difficult and destruction is easy. For example, the construction of temples, cathedrals, and castles takes years, sometimes decades, but a bomb destroys all beauty in the fraction of a second it takes to explode. The same thing can happen with people. It takes years of hard labor from parents, grandparents, friends, teachers, and neighbors to make a good person; however, one bullet can destroy that person's life. Furthermore, you can build good relations for years, but one wrong step—

a scandal, for instance—can eliminate all the good. As a case in point, destruction of trust is a one-time event.

Creation from this point of view is achieving harmony and finding a way for many parts to work together. This is the way to "cosmos," as the ancient Greeks said. Figuratively speaking, creation (harmony) needs tuning, ear training, organizing, and delicate work. Destruction, on the other hand, is a way to chaos—no special skills are needed. Any person can take a hammer and destroy the world's most beautiful sculpture. Naturally, the way down is easier than the way up.

Conclusion one: Creative communication creates relations and leads to success, while requiring energy, work, and love of people.

Conclusion two: Destructive communication destroys relations and leads to failure, but it is easy. If a person employs destructive communication, he might be:

- ignorant (does not know ethical norms and conversational rules)
- untrained (knows the rules, but cannot use them properly)
- careless (knows the rules and can use them, but does not care)
- sick (knows the rules and can use them, but has no energy or healthy thinking)
- disruptive or criminally oriented (knows the rules and can use them, but breaks them on purpose)

Now that you know what creative communication is, it's time to see how it starts and what it includes. Here you will begin to see how your creative communi-

cation (positive, supportive, and inspiring) will build
an environment that will make your creative and innovative efforts much more productive.

WHERE DOES CREATIVE COMMUNICATION BEGIN?

Creative communication begins on the same level as any
communication, on the most basic communication level
known to science—nonverbal.

Have you noticed that you can say awful things in a
loving and intimate manner, and nobody gets hurt or of-
fended? On the other hand, if you choose the most loving
words and hiss them or speak them sarcastically, just wait
for the negative reaction.

This is what I call "the paradox of nonverbal dominance," or "ParONDo" for short. ParONDo is easy to understand if you look at the animal (prehuman) world. Nonverbal communication exists everywhere: in threats, in
stances, in birds' dances, and so on. The scientific view
of the world estimates the age of human existence as
about three to seven million years and the age of prehuman live matter as billions of years old. Nonverbal behavior, therefore, is much deeper in history and much more
ingrained in our genes and subconscious minds. So, when
it comes to comparing verbal stimuli with nonverbal stimuli, the nonverbal dominates.

Moreover, there is experimental evidence of the dominance of nonverbal over verbal. People, as you know, can
easily lie with words. However, unless people have been
trained or practice a lot, it is much more difficult for them
to deceive a person nonverbally. Once, prison inmates were

asked to tell lies using gestures of openness—surprisingly, they couldn't do it, or they had difficulties doing it.

Furthermore, 86 percent of a person's credibility is based on one's nonverbal communication. Some authors even believe that up to 93 percent of our communication is nonverbal, and only 7 percent of information is conveyed by words. Conflict Theory states that *all* conflicts have one cause—the discrepancy between human self-evaluation and the social evaluation of that human. Simply stated, *all conflicts happen due to lack of love.* Love, though, requires more than a word expression—it needs action. Nonverbal communication is the most significant part of this action.

Therefore, if we are going to learn creative communication, we should start this learning with nonverbal communication exercises. There is a pressing need to teach people positive nonverbal behavior. Dr. Kerry Johnson, a famous psychologist and speaker, for example, offers an interesting course called "How to Read Clients' Minds." However, it is not enough to start this training with adults in business, in education, and in the general public. It must begin in grade school, or even earlier, if we want to raise creators, not destroyers.

In my classes, I usually teach specific exercises that work on Kinesics (gestures and mimics), Proxemics (distances and zones between communicators), Chronemics (time of contact or communication), and Paralanguage (intonations, pitch, volume).

QUICK FIXES

Changes in nonverbal communication change the whole person. They are visible. They immediately send visual clues to other people. Sometimes, it is enough to change just a little, and the results will be far better.

Let me present some obvious cases that make my point clear:

Case 1

Jeremy was a very tall teenager. He towered over his peers. When he was sitting, his natural desire was to sit as low as possible so that his head was level with the other students. The way he did this on his chair was to stretch: to put his legs as far forward as possible and to move his shoulders as far back as possible. His hands automatically crossed in front of his chest, and his legs crossed, too. His head bent forward or fell on the side when he was tired. His eyes moved away.

This is what an observer, such as a teacher, saw when he looked at Jeremy in class.

Here is what the observer felt and thought:

- Crossed arms, crossed legs—blocks on the body. Neutral meaning: protection. However, there are some negative meanings: indifference, hostility, desire not to be touched, desire to cut communication.
- Body bent back: no interest, desire to be as far from the teacher as possible.
- Head bent forward or falling aside: aggression and indifference.

In addition, all these physical gestures signaled the brain that it was naptime, and Jeremy began to nod. The teacher became frustrated and angry. He asked a question and called on Jeremy. Jeremy couldn't answer. Did Jeremy earn a good grade in the class? Obviously not. Furthermore, Jeremy set an example for other students, and if his behavior was not confronted, the whole class would soon be sleeping. As a result of his low grades and behavioral problems, Jeremy was kicked out of class and found himself on the street. He turned to drugs, was arrested by the police, and finally was sent to the Center for Youth on Chemical Dependencies in hope that sixty days of special education would return him to a more beneficial school life. This is the place where I met Jeremy—in a class of fifteen other teenagers having drug problems.

After explanation and demonstration it took only several minutes to correct the situation. Jeremy changed his body position into one that expresses attention, readiness to work, interest, and a positive attitude. The results, were stunning. He was alert for the two days of the workshop. His answers were timely and correct. He had no behavior problems, and teachers who were also present at the workshop thought he was doing much better.

The simplicity of the creative communication solution is amazing. It is also amazing how scary and unfair the consequences of destructive communication can be: jail for a nonverbal behavior mistake!

Case 2

I was conducting a seminar at a company with which I've worked for many years. During the lunch break, I heard a voice call, "Dr. Andy!" I turned to see Becky X. She told me a story about how, after one of my seminars, she talked to her stepdaughter about nonverbal communication techniques and about my promise to make a child an A-student very quickly. They laughed together, but her stepdaughter decided to try. The next quarter she was on the dean's list. She told her friend about it, and the next quarter her friend was on the dean's list, too. "Wow!" I said, "Thank you for sharing! Let's go to the group of managers that I teach now and share this news." She did, and I'm sure many other parents and grandparents followed the simple instructions for making their siblings A-students. Let's look at these techniques.

TECHNIQUES TO CREATE OPENNESS

To help my students learn to be open, I created a powerful method called MANDO (Method of Applied Nonverbal DOminance) that produces openness. I say "powerful" because it changes not only thinking, but the whole personality as well. It makes people better learners, better communicators, and much happier people.

In my classes, I ask students to make a circle around me and then, suddenly, I say, "Freeze!" They freeze. I point to their postures and to the way they hold their arms. I point to arm locks and hand locks (front and back), leg locks, foot locks (any crossed arms, feet, legs)—I ask them what it means. They are puzzled. I explain that these locks are a means of protection or defense. Defense and protection are good sometimes, but when they become a habit, we forget about them and continue to live with the habitual locks on our bodies. If during classes our bodies are locked up, then instead of feeling new feelings and getting new information, we sit behind our own thick walls and fences. As a result, most of the knowledge you came for passes you by—you pay for sitting rather than for learning. Such studying is very ineffective. So if you want to make it more efficient, begin with opening yourself—get rid of locks or blocks.

Listening

Being open also means being open to people—to their views, their needs, their passions, and even their mistakes. Being open is the same as being forgiving, accepting, and tolerant. Being open means listening to others and trying to understand their pain, their hopes, their dreams. Being open is being humane. It means to accept others as equals worthy of your humanity.

If you take only one idea from this book, take this one: Be open. Not only will that approach to life help you be more creative, it also will allow your many ideas to shine in a positive light. Your ideas help others, or they will be mindful of the needs of others. Frankly speaking, the world as a whole could be better if we all took this approach to life. There would be fewer wars, less trouble, less cruelty, and less hatred. Being open means MegaValuing people—they are valuable beyond all measures. This is the Fourth Law of MegaCreativity.

Being open means listening. Be ready to listen and ready to accept. The art of active listening seemingly belongs to nonverbal communication, though it already involves some verbal communication. However, before the words, there is paralanguage we have to learn to listen to. Paralanguage includes:

- volume of speech (loud/quiet)
- pitch of speech (high/low)

- speed of speech (from zero to four hundred words per minute)
- special characteristics of speech such as accents and pronunciation habits

These features, if you'll excuse the pun, speak louder than words. We all react to loudness, to pitch, to speed, and even to accents. We react to these features sooner than we react to the words themselves.

Listening is a fine art, so learning to listen is as hard as learning any other art. During my classes, we have numerous exercises on listening. If you try to match a person's volume, pitch, speed, and accent, you at once will be a better listener. Listening can be creative or destructive. While actively listening and showing interest in what is said, you create a wonderful atmosphere of openness.

Let's discuss some special exercises that can help you.

Beach Listening: Beach listening is an exercise for training your listening abilities when you are bored or have nothing to do. At the beach, we normally listen to the people nearby. The task is to select the farthest person you can hear instead of the closest one; tune your ear, and try to understand what the person is saying. This exercise trains your physical abilities to hear and your mental abilities to recognize. Of course, you don't have to be at the beach to try this exercise. You can do it in any public place. I call it "beach listening" because at the beach we have time to spare that can be used for training. It's not an easy exercise, but the most difficult tasks often have the most benefits.

TV Un-Tuning: TV (or radio) un-tuning is another good technique. Turn the volume on your radio or television as low as possible while still being able to hear it. Focus on the voices, straining to hear what they're saying. In today's world, we enjoy technology that allows us to hear clear voices in movies and on television, radio, and telephones. Our lives, as a result, are easier, but these technologies can make us lazy listeners. By turning down the volume or by tuning your radio so that the channel doesn't come through clearly, we can learn to be better listeners.

Jamming the Gem: Jamming the gem requires a group of people, such as in a classroom or in a seminar at work. First, break the group into two smaller groups with equal numbers. Choose partners so that every member of the first group has a partner in the second group. Seat the first group on one side of a room and the second group on the other side. Ask members of the first group to dictate figures or letters (in random order) to their partners in the second group. The partner must jot down the specific message he or she hears. The noise from everyone talking simultaneously is jamming the gem of information needed by each listening participant. To unjam the gem, the brain must tune out all the noises except the one voice needed. This is a fun activity that trains the brain to focus and listen.

You can create many exercises like these. *You* are the

creator of your trained brain, so create your own difficulties. In addition to learning to listen in a focused way, you will also train your openness—your desire to listen—despite all the difficulties. Oh, how this skill is needed!

CREATIVE VERBAL COMMUNICATION

The next level of communication you have to work on is verbal communication. Creative verbal communication includes all positive or at least neutral phrases that serve the purpose of continuing communication.

Case 1

A simple example of creative communication is illustrated by the following experiment. Ask a person whether she likes flowers, wait for a positive answer, and then sharply say that you don't like them. That stops the conversation immediately because *a negative answer is destructive communication.*

Case 2

In the second case, ask a person if she likes flowers and, having received a positive answer, say that you like them, too. Ask further which flowers she likes most. If the answer is roses, say you like roses, too. Ask what colors the person likes best, and so on. Continue to find similarities and "coincidences." This will create a good mood, continuing conversation, and, most important, the desire on both sides to communicate further. This is a pure example of creative communication.

CREATIVITY ON COMMUNICATION LEVEL

The practical rule for creative communication is to reduce or even avoid negative statements (following our Second Law). I often give my students the assignment to avoid *no* and *not* for at least two weeks. This changes their lives dramatically.

One more rule is to include positive, reinforcing phrases in your activities. For example, use phrases such as: "Good job." "Nicely done." "Superb work." "We are really fortunate to have you on the team!" "It must be exciting to be so creative!"

By following these simple rules for verbal communication, you can create much better relations with people around you. Creativity, as you see, is present on the level of communication, too. Apparently if we want to make a person much more creative, we must also work on this level. Otherwise, it would be like trying to heavily renovate the top floor of a remodeled house without enhancing and redoing the lower floors. Creativity must be present in the entire building from foundation to rooftop.

Since discovering that, we have devised the ideal structure of the course and the ideal structure of the lesson. Now, in every seminar or workshop, students go to the existential level first and learn creative existence. Then they climb the level of communication (the second level) and learn creative communication. After that, they learn creative methods and techniques, which belong to the third, instrumental level. This all gives an enormous boost of creativity on the fourth level, which forms the foundation for the innovation level (the fifth level).

SUPEREFFECTIVE COMMUNICATION

Generally speaking, approximately 20 to 30 percent of people communicate at the level of subeffective communication; approximately 50 to 60 percent communicate at the level of effective communication; and approximately 10 to 20 percent communicate at the level of supereffective communication. Supersuccessful individuals communicate at this higher level of communication. These people are our leaders, stars, or geniuses, but seldom is their success attributed directly to supereffective communication.

An example of one of these individuals can be found in an article in *The Chronicle of Higher Education* (June 16, 1995), that describes how Cornell University President Frank Rhodes helped raise $1.25 billion for the university and was deemed a "Fund-raising Master." The article emphasized his highly developed communication skills: his personal touch; his British accent; his tireless passion for Cornell; his philosophy of "creating the future"; his intense interest in people; his memory for names and faces; his daily writing of thank-you notes to people he had met that day; his file of interesting quotes, anecdotes, and jokes, which he relied on for speeches; and, finally, his energetic, good-natured character, which allowed him to travel, to meet and greet people, and to have fun at his job. He was, without question, a master of communication.

Ask yourself:

- Do you write thank-you notes to people you meet or who do you even the smallest favor?
- Are you trained to memorize names and faces?
- Do you keep a catalog of jokes, anecdotes, and stories?

- Do you have a passion for what you are doing?
- Do you have an attractive philosophy for people to be fascinated by?

If not, then you know what to start doing. This will make you a supereffective communicator with extreme creative capabilities.

Add to this all exercises on intelligence and speed-reading, on making a perfect speech in one minute, and on writing a winning composition (what I teach in my classes), and your flight up will be very fast. So create your future. Communicate creatively! To be a creative communicator, love people. Open your heart to all the millions of varieties in human images, races, cultures, languages, and views. Become MegaOpen. Have positive and exciting goals. Learn and practice! Practice! Practice!

Chapter Twelve

Employ MegaPowerful Tools

Language in and of itself is a treasure beyond measure.

ALEANDR

After learning and practicing the basics of creative communication, students become so different that climbing to the next level—the level of creative instruments—is much easier. If your mind is open and your communication channels are open, then you are ready for the voyage to the planet Genius. On this voyage you will learn the methods and techniques that make geniuses geniuses.

This chapter will teach you some powerful thinking tools (intellectual methodologies) that will allow you to solve problems with vigor, originality, passion, fun, and outstanding results.

Believe it or not, you have already learned the fundamental method that leads to MegaCreativity. Get ready for a surprise.

This method is the language that you speak.

Since you acquired language, you have learned

- enormous numbers of creative thoughts (words created by others before you).

- large numbers of grammatical and stylistic patterns to create words and combinations of words, and to express what is most important.
- some ways for creating creative thoughts.

Language allows us to create and re-create thoughts, to express and reexpress ideas, emotions, intentions, attitudes, etc. Language is the most powerful tool ever. Use it and pay gratitude to those who created this MegaPowerful tool.

When you learned language, you actually stepped into a culture that creates and re-creates itself in speech every day. You stepped into the culture of creativity, worshiped creativity, called creativity, practiced creativity, and multiplied creativity. This culture is the culture of speech (in linguistic terms) and freedom of speech (in political terms).

In this chapter, we will start with the method that is derived from the language—from your ability to use, combine, and think of words.

METHOD OF RANDOM WORDS

Method of random words is one of the simplest methods you can use to increase creativity, and the authors of it are lost in time. In my opinion, it is as old as the language itself. It may have a different name. Edward De Bono, a celebrated author in creativity, calls it word provocation and lateral thinking; many practitioners call it the method of forced relations; and Max Fisher even makes it fishing-oriented and calls it "IdeaFisher."

No matter how this ancient method is introduced, the

fact is that our lazy (energy-saving) minds are staying in the hole; when faced with a problem, they tend to choose the beaten path—the closest words that are habitually used every day. This is less creative. It certainly takes additional effort to reach for the higher and less obvious (non-associated) words. It takes *your* energy, but it is definitely more creative. A random word actually makes your mind move away from your most lazy position. Here is why it becomes more creative.

There are many models of creativity, but you can certainly remember and use the simplest, and to some extent universal, model. It has two stages: the search for a big idea (like a deviation from the beaten path) and the application of the big idea to your problem.

So, in essence, a word taken randomly from a dictionary, book, or friend diverts the mind from the beaten path. When applied to the problem, it makes the solution much more creative. The Method of Random Words can double or triple your creativity in several minutes. It also leads to MegaCreativity, but we'll cover this later.

Let's practice. Here is a group of objects: chair, bed, car, any object. Take the first one—chair. If you think about improving the chair, then your thoughts are probably focused on "sitting." Also, nearly automatically, your mind goes to making the chair larger, softer, or more comfortable. These are typical ideas. All people go through them at once when the problem of inventing a new chair is presented. To make a creative leap, take a random word, apply it to your problem, and get out of the system.

As an example, take these random words: cabbage, telescope, consumable, camel, beyond, tractor, just, abbreviation, atomic, interval, truncated, counterpoint, go, venture, eliminate, burger, needle, listen, launch, tribune, dynamite, extricate, animal, me, adventure, balloon, camouflage.

Choose one of them. Let's take the first word *cabbage.*

Cabbage

What does it have to do with the chair? Nothing. A less creative brain would say, "Let's go to another word!" That would be a mistake. The essence of the method is in connecting this random word with the object you are thinking about, so it is a must. Try again!

What are the characteristics of a cabbage?

It has leaves. These leaves conform to each other, and they are layered. Can chairs be made like that? Aha! Stacked chairs! When you don't need them, you stack them one on top of each other. It means the inner form of one chair is equal to the outer form of the other chair. Perhaps the person who first thought of stackable chairs was using a cabbage or a salad as a design model! Now, when you can see that it worked once, why not try and find another technical solution?

Another use is differently sized chairs—small chairs fitting into the bigger ones, and all chairs fitting into the largest chair. In this case, a big family with a big father, a normal-sized mother, and five average-sized children would stack all the chairs into one, put them into the trunk, and go for a picnic. A lot of room saved!

Here is the third idea. Imagine a medically clean chair, every layer of which can be peeled off and thrown away after each patient. No need to wash the chair or put a cover on it.

Aha! You got it! Thanks to the word *cabbage*, now we have the difference!

Let's take another example!

Telescope

Telescope? Chair? What is your first reaction? It's ridiculous! But let's try it. It will be fun. The world of imagination and creativity is much more fun than the real world because everything is allowed.

What qualities of a telescope can we use? First of all, it magnifies objects. Secondly, a part of it slides in and out. Is it possible to make a chair using that feature? Normally chairs are rigid or fixed. Can we make handles or legs height-adjustable? Is that possible? Wouldn't it be nice to have a chair that could stand straight on a slope? For fishing and hunting? For painting landscapes? Just make the back legs smaller and the front legs taller— that's it! Wow!

Where did these ideas come from? From a seemingly ridiculous random word!

The difference between a low-creative mind and a highly-creative mind is that the latter says "yes" and looks for new combinations, while the former says "no" and stops. We are highly creative minds, aren't we? So let us take one more challenge.

Consumable

What is your first reaction? "No way!" right? That is how our traditional, inertial, lazy, or energy-saving brains protest against the necessity to work.

Let's step over it and try. Let's choose the creative journey! For instance, if you are in the arctic zone, or in space travel where the carried load is limited, the danger of hunger is real. I bet you would love to have some unusual reserves. Edible furniture is a must for a long space trip. In case of extreme need (a meteorite destroys the food compartment, a bear eats all the provisions), you would be able to boil your chair legs like chicken and have a delicious soup! Wouldn't it be better than dying? Or, what if it was consumable, as in "used up"? Chairs that disintegrate when you're done with them. No waste. That would be ideal for wilderness travelers. They go to a remote area to camp, unfold their chairs, and when they're ready to leave, the chairs turn to dust! Consumable chairs—you don't have to carry them back!

After you've made your chair cabbage-like, telescopic-folding, and chicken-tasting, do you think you could have done it without random words? Right! Here is the value. As you remember, I promised to double or triple your creativity rate. Here it is: Every word helps you produce two to three more ideas, and they are two or three times more creative. In a mathematical sense, we multiplied your creativity four to nine times, but let it be two to three. We aren't greedy.

What are the potentials and limits of the method of random words? A dictionary is a potential. Thousands of words (one million in the English language), and no limits for a creative mind! So here you are. You have a million words to use as diversions from the beaten path. Here is your chance to move to MegaCreativity. After some days and weeks of practice, the words you choose will be remembered and—never mind which objects you apply them to—your decisions will seem creative to others. (They do not have to know that you use a method.)

Check it. Apply the word *cabbage* to your homework assignment, to your car, to your bookshelf. New ideas are coming, right? So by having ten to twenty random words ready for deviation at any time, you teach your mind to make this move automatically. Thus, higher creativity becomes a part of your everyday life.

An example: Imagine you are a teacher, and you need a funny exercise to make students study or review some formulas for a physics test. Mentally, you pull out the list of words from your memory, choose, for example, the word *telescope,* and begin to think how to use a telescope (or its features) to motivate students to learn. In a couple of minutes, you make up a new class activity. You write all the formulas on a small, round sheet of paper (like a planet), and hang it on the board. The text is so small that it is unreadable by the naked eye from the students' seats. You introduce the rules: Each member of the two (or three) teams is allowed to use the telescope, which you have brought and placed in the center of the room, only once for two or three seconds. Just like in life, time is limited. The task of the team is to make a complete list of formulas from your sheet. Those who manage to write all the formulas win. In an evening extracurricular event, you could allow them to see the moon and real planets through this telescope. I bet you will have a lot of fun, and I bet your students will learn the formulas.

Would you like to try an idea by yourself? Suppose your friend is coming from far away. You have not seen him for a year, and you need a nice surprise. The random word you will be working with can be taken from the previous list.

Do it here.

_____

_____

_____

_____

_____

The method of random words has its strong points and weak points. It can be applied to any situation (this is good), but as you see it is random in its essence. Who knows which solution is the best? So, use it when there is an open-ended activity or when many answers are acceptable.

The method of random words is only one of approximately two hundred available methods. However, we will not study all of them—that is up to you. Check literature, Web sites, and university courses on creativity. We will study only the most interesting and promising methods.

METHOD OF METAPHORS

This method also deals with words. I call it the *method of metaphors*.

Metaphors appear everywhere in literature, and research literature on metaphors is almost endless. Poets, writers, and readers love metaphors. People often don't think there is a method for creating metaphors, though. They think only people who are talented and gifted can produce metaphors. A famous Russian writer, Yury Olesha, once said, "After us, only metaphors stay in the history." There is great truth in that because successful metaphors continue to live in the language long after their authors disappear.

It certainly works better when a person is talented or gifted, but what methodologists (and I am one of them) try to do is analyze how the result can be achieved without smoke and mirrors. (What is a talent? What is a gift? A gift from whom? Get talented in an hour, get gifted in a day—show your ability, and people will say you are talented and gifted.)

There are several models for building metaphors. I tried some of them and found this to be the simplest one—let's call it Model A.

Simile (*like, as*) ➜ Metaphor (without *like, as*)

This common method shows that you can easily go from a simile to a metaphor: "He is *like* a disaster" ➜ "He is a disaster." "She is *like* a ham" ➜ "She is a ham."

The method I created is more complex, but it is also more poetic. Let's call it Model B. In its essence the method uses analytical diversion to create an original synthesis later. We analyze (disassemble) things and then synthesize (assemble) them anew. There are two main features in the metaphor: the form and the contents. One of the most widely used forms is "the noun (N_1) of noun (N_2)." For example, a typical row of metaphors runs like this: "I open the door (N_1) of my dream (N_2) and enter the room of my memories. Here, on the walls of the past, I see the canvases of my loves and sorrows. Painted with the strokes of doubts and exhalations, these canvases stayed the monuments of gone dreams, the sculptures of events that no longer exist."

First, check whether this quoted text reads more interesting than the following: "I remember my house with lots of old portraits." Second, find and underline the structure "the N_1 of N_2" in this text, and you will see that all of the metaphors use the same model.

The next step in building a model is to understand what type of nouns fits the N_1 category and what type of nouns fits the N_2 category. This is where we go from form to contents. Not all nouns can be used in these two positions to make a metaphor. For example, if you put *leg* into position N_1 and *table* into position N_2, then the resulting expression "the leg of the table" isn't a metaphor. Something is wrong. Another example: Put the noun *dream* into position N_1 and the noun *table* into position N_2. As a result, it becomes "the dream of my table"—interesting, but not a metaphor.

Analysis shows that nouns in the position N_1 must have the meanings of objects. They must be tangible—or, they must belong to the material world. They must be touchable, visible, observable, or just material. On the contrary, nouns in the position N_2 must belong to the ideal world. They must denote something intangible—feelings, emotions, perceptions, ideas, thoughts, memories, and so on.

To practice separating the material and ideal worlds, please create a table that looks like the one below:

Material World Nouns	Ideal World Nouns

While working with material nouns, consider four kinds of matter: solid, liquid, gas, and plasma. The traditional example of plasma is flame. Ask yourself for some examples of solid matter, then ask yourself for examples of liquid matter. Fill in the gaps. When you finish the material side, write the types of ideal nouns on the ideal side. Or, fill in both sides of the table as the types occur to you. Open your mind and scribble both types of nouns as quickly as you can.

After you finish the table, begin to make metaphors. Make at least five of them. You probably will end up with something like the following: *the waves of my love, the oxygen of her faith, the rays of his hopes.*

Now, use these metaphors to make sentences. If they

turn into a story, that's even better. I'm sure your sentences or your story is different from what you would have written without metaphors. Metaphors are so powerful that they lead imagination after them. That is why poets often find one metaphor, and it becomes the beginning or ending of a poem.

This method, just like other methods, has its strong points and weak points. Strong point: It has no limits—it is open. Weak point: It's great for literature, advertising, and teaching, but it is less effective for inventions and technology.

METHOD OF FOUR DELAYS FOR GENIUS WAYS (4DELAYS4GENIUSWAYS)

In addition to working with words, some readers prefer to work with numbers. Let's look at a powerful method for using numerical thinking. Earlier we discussed genius methods of thinking, and one of the main characteristics was withholding the answer—trying to go deeper than the obvious. For this purpose, I use this method to delay coming up with an answer at least four times.

I am explaining this method here for the first time, so from this moment, you are the owner of a unique opportunity. Learn it today—use it today—and your decisions will be dramatically different.

To understand how it works, look back at the first problem in chapter one ("put a dot somewhere on the page"). Recall your first idea. I bet it was something like, "Hey, who cares? Let me do it fast." Is that right? Well, look what would happen if you delayed placing the dot.

	Expression	**Action**	**Reaction**
First idea (desire)	"Hey, who cares? Let me do it fast."	Put it in the middle of the circle.	"This could be too easy, too traditional."
Second idea (desire)	"Okay—middle is too obvious, but let me put it somewhere else."	Put it away from the center and closer to the side.	"Well, this may be better, but is it the best!"
Third idea (desire)	"Did he say in the circle or out of the circle? Why not *on* the circle?	Put it on the circle—just on the line.	"Hmm . . . pretty interesting. Why not farther?"
Fourth idea (desire)	"What if I put it out of the circle?"	Put it out of the circle.	"It is still on this side of the paper. What if I can be more original?"
Fifth idea (desire)	"What if I turn the page over and . . ."	Put it on the other side.	"Wow! That's neat! That's a genius! I'm still on the page (within the task), but I'm away from the trivial."

Do you see how the delay leads to a new solution? This is a formal pattern that can be trained—the pattern of deferred (delayed?) answer, the pattern of four-step deviation (leading to the fifth level), the pattern of forced thinking that will launch the quality of your solution over the others.

The trouble with our untrained thinking is that we seem to be in a hurry to give the answer, as if one second counts more than eternity. Sometimes it's okay, but a habit of doing it makes us superficial and trivial. If you would like to check, you could see that Karl Gauss in his solution (on page 59) went through the same four delays to the fifth step. Louis Pasteur went through the same four delays to a fifth step, which proved to be a genius solution. So, Four Delays for Genius Ways (4Delays4GeniusWays) is a neat method to learn and to use. When put into words it sounds very simple: Before you act, consider taking four more steps in the same direction. This method teaches you to value the distant or deeper ideas, and also the thinking process that leads to them.

VALUE EVERYONE'S IDEAS AND YOU'LL VALUE YOUR OWN

I hope that in this section you have learned or relearned the importance of valuing people in the creative process. Value others and value yourself, try to communicate in fresh ways with fresh language, and you will continue your journey toward becoming a MegaCreator. To end this chapter and this section, let's look at one more creativity method that focuses on creative communication and valuing people.

The method known as *ship council* originated centuries ago, and its inventors are lost in history. However, it is still a powerful method and one that places value on everyone's ideas. It is an early form of brainstorming, in which the generation of ideas is not controlled, but the expression of the ideas is controlled by a rule: the lowest-ranking (age) person starts, and then the sequence of answers is determined by the increasing rank (age). If you use this method at work, the person lowest in the organizational hierarchy offers ideas first, then the next person on the ladder up, and so on. If you use this method in a classroom or seminar, begin with the youngest person and move sequentially to the oldest person.

This method originated on ships at sea. When a captain needed ideas from his crew to solve a particular problem, a meeting was called and the youngest or lowest-ranking sailor would offer an idea first, followed by the next youngest or lowest, and on up to the captain's highest-ranking assistants.

The strong point of this method is that it delays authority, pressure, and criticism. This prevents unintended or intended idea suppression by higher-ranking or older personnel. Younger or lower-ranking members of the group do not feel obligated to agree with superiors, because the superiors have not yet had a turn to speak. Moreover, superiors have time and the opportunity to find a better idea. This method also has weak points: The number of ideas is limited by the number of participants because the hierarchy has been established, and a second round of ideas is either impossible or will be influenced by the ideas of higher-ranking individuals.

I am fond of this method, because it gives equal importance to everyone's ideas. This approach embodies the essence of creative communication and MegaValuing people. Everyone is important. Everyone's ideas are valuable. Everyone's way of expressing ideas is valuable, too—any language, any dialect, any accent. If you use this approach in your life, you will be a more positive person and, as we discussed earlier, that positive energy will make you more creative. It also will help you avoid being too critical of your own ideas. Give yourself the same respect and generosity you extend to everyone in your group, whether it's with colleagues at work, classmates at school, or family members at home. This attitude is crucial in your journey to becoming a MegaCreator. Now that we have covered it, let's move on to the next step.

Launch to the Genius Orbit

A person may die, nations may rise and fall, but an
idea lives on. Ideas have endurance without death.

JOHN F. KENNEDY

This section is about our methodology applied to life, to
business and education, and to our everyday programs
and problems. This section tells you what to do with your
new abilities and skills, and shows you how you can apply
them to the problems around you—not artificial, not just
learning problems, but real-world problems and real
tasks—in other words, how you can use MegaCreativity.
It is faster than creativity, but so what? Yes, it is the new
era of understanding creativity. So what? What are the
consequences? What are the perspectives? What are the
practical steps to utilizing it, and how can it help you in
today's and tomorrow's job, studies, social life, and family
life? This final section will give you some answers to these
questions.

Chapter Thirteen

Master the Methods of Geniuses

We have to regard it as our sacred responsibility to unfold and develop each individual's creative ability as dim as the spark may be and kindle it to whatever flame it may conceivably develop.

VICTOR LOWENFELD

In the previous chapter, we looked at ways to increase your creative power through specific methods and techniques. In this chapter, we'll look at more of these methods, and we'll go further: We will try to show to you that even the best of them (as instruments of our thinking) can be improved.

The logic is simple: If you learn how to think like Leonardo da Vinci (see the wonderful book by Michael J. Gelb, *How to Think Like Leonardo da Vinci*, 1998) or even like Jesus (see the extraordinary book of Kobus Neethling, Hennie Stander, and Raché Rutherford, *Think Like Jesus*, 2000), you will master only two ways of thinking. How about Socrates? Aristotle? Plato? Galileo? Newton? Kepler? Rembrandt? Shakespeare? Hegel? Einstein? How about hundreds and thousands of other geniuses?

Are you able to study them all? Are there books on *how*

they thought? Is repeating their patterns of thinking enough?

The winning strategy (methodology) is the following: Choose the best, learn it, improve it, orient it to your own problem, and use it. In this chapter, you'll find techniques from our School of Geniuses and how we adapted the techniques to improve our own situations.

BRAINSTORMING ("BRAINSTO")

The essence of Alex F. Osborn's brainstorming method is the following: People sit around, and when the problem is stated, they begin to throw out ideas, which are captured either by writing or by recording. All ideas are accepted, and no criticism is allowed during the first stage. During the second stage, all ideas are checked by another group of people or are selected and developed by the original group. You can find a description of brainstorming in numerous books starting with Alex F. Osborn's *Applied Imagination* and finishing with the latest "modern" versions, like *Brainstorm Alone: The Creative Problem Solving Tape*—a variant of brainstorming on tape.

Improvement

Brainstorming, due to its success, engendered a large number of variants, including reverse brainstorming. So as a continuation of the trend, I also introduced my own version. I call it Branching Out Brainstorming (BOB). You can do it when the audience is large. When each new feature (color, size, shape, etc.) appears in discussions, it is given to a "branching out" group which "grows" only this particular branch while a larger audience continues the general process. At the end, the number of variants is much higher than in normal brainstorming because it is the product of multiplication of all the branches. This improvement increased the number of ideas.

This is the way we look at the methods with our geniuses: Learn the essence, master, improve, and apply. Here are the methods used in our school. The description is very brief (for more information, see the many other books on creative problem solving).

METHODS FROM OUR SCHOOL OF GENIUSES
Morphological Analysis ("Morpho")

In Greek, the word "morph-" meant "form." "Logos" meant "word" which later became "study of." So in grammar, for example, morphology, as opposed to syntax, means cutting words into pieces and analyzing their forms. In Biology, it means dissecting animals into parts and studying these parts separately. Therefore, in creative thinking, before idea generation, the object that needs to be improved is mentally divided into parts, and only after that, is brainstorming applied to separate parts. Generation of ideas is now directed by the morphological matrix or table.

For example, you need to invent a new toy. Make a table like the one below, and put whatever characteristics you want into the headings.

Toy	bright	light	moving	talking
mechanical				
chemical				
biological				

Then on the cross sections of rows and columns you must find and develop a toy having both characteristics. According to this particular table, it will be "a mechanical bright toy," "a mechanical light toy," "a mechanical moving toy," etc. Many of the versions, as you see, will be of little interest, but some of them can click an interesting idea. Look at the cross section of "chemical" and "light." Somebody thought of it and made plastic tubes that radiate light because of a chemical reaction inside—not because of an electrical charge. Children have fun with these during evening parties and events.

Improvement: Certainly, the most powerful improvement of this approach is the morphological matrix that we showed in chapter five—our BAMMA—the methodology that leads to millions of ideas.

Morphological analysis (and synthesis) produces many more ideas than any brainstorming (pure free association). Ideas are precisely placed in the table and, therefore, are not lost. Idea generation, as a process, is definitely separated from idea manifestation because the verbalizing of ideas can be done later. This compresses the process and, as a result, this method helps to achieve the level of more than one hundred ideas per minute.

Focal Object ("FocO")

The essence of the method is in its name. The object you need to change (improve or invent) is placed in the focus of attention and new features (expressed by adjectives) are applied to it. Here is how it works.

Usually, the name of the object is written on the board.

The leader of a creative session asks participants to make up seven nouns and writes them on the board around the center. The leader asks the group to make up seven adjectives for every noun, and then students apply the found adjectives to the original object, which is standing in the focus.

Focal Object allows people to make many divergent moves by introducing two additional operations: (1) listing nouns and (2) listing adjectives. This is a structured activity that loosens the mind. As a result, in half an hour, the group has $7 \times 7 \times 3 = 147$ (i.e., about 150 ideas) for a focal object. You can certainly use this method for developing new ideas for a party, lesson, gift, etc.

Improvement: In my modification of the method, we first make up nouns, then collect adjectives. Only after this is done, do I introduce the object to change. It allows participants to generate more diverse adjectives (they are not oriented yet). Also, in order to avoid oversimplified adjectives like "good," "interesting," "large," I ask participants to give me the fourth adjective coming to their mind (omitting the first three because they are traditionally trivial). This strengthens the pool of adjectives as well.

Personal Analogy ("PersonAna")

Introduced by William J.J. Gordon, Personal Analogy asks you to think about an object or problem as if it is yourself.

For example, take any object and make a story starting with words: "I am a (this object)." If you have to invent, for instance, a table, your story could start like this: "I am a table. I am solid and firm. I have many brothers and sisters around me in the class. I like teamwork. As a rule, I have at least one other member in my team—this is a chair. Since I do not like to be alone, I would like to have a permanent connection with my chair . . . " Aha, here is the first new idea—to make a chair attached to the table that's moving around but always connected.

Improvement: I care more about people than about inventions. I allow my students to become the most stupid things possible for them to have fun: a tail of the elephant, a wing of the fly, a splash of water. One little girl from my School of Geniuses liked this method because it provides an original point of view. She used it for her compositions and won many contests.

Symbolic Analogy ("SymbolAna")
Symbolic Analogy works with symbols (words, letters, phrases, figures, pictures, etc.—not the objects).

Improvement: I use this name for a cluster of methods dealing with symbols. For example, I teach the so-called NonScientific Cut. It works because objects are not equal to their names. Names are arbitrary—their sound form is normally not connected with the objects they denote. That is why one and the same object—table—is called "der Tisch" in German, "stol" in Russian, "table" in English. These arbitrary relations give some freedom to the working mind. It can operate with symbols instead of objects and then go back to objects.

As one excited parent in our school told me, her small

child asked, "Why are there so many ministers in the government and not a single maxister?" In the child's question, one can see the NonScientific Cut because a child cuts the word "nonscientifically" into "mini" and "sters" and contrasts "mini" to "maxi" like in miniskirt and maxiskirt. Numerous examples can be viewed in the newspaper cartoons where, for instance, Dennis the Menace asks, "If kids have kidneys, do bugs have bugneys?"

Actually, when used to the limit, this powerful method leads to LinguaHeuristic—discovering new things in the material world with the help of the language.

Fantastic Analogy ("FantastAna")

Fantastic Analogy diverts one's thinking by means of using magic objects and processes. For example, most everybody knows the following famous magic objects: Aladdin's lamp, an invisible hat (making a person invisible when put on), a flying carpet (which can fly without an engine or wings), etc. So if you have to improve an object or a process, think of what it would do if it were magic. For instance, what would the magic shoelace do? One of my students offered to make a "healthy" shoelace, and when we asked in surprise how a shoelace could be healthy, he explained, "It will untie itself all the time for an overweight person to do his bending and thus train during the day." What would the magic socks do? Another student's answer: treat feet with hidden medicine. What would the magic steering wheel do? Make a sudden bump when the driver is falling asleep. These seemingly "magic" actions, when developed into technical decisions, can lead to real inventions.

Improvement: You may remember the method of Ideal Final Result (IFR) that appeared when you worked with BAMMA. Actually, the Ideal Final Result in BAMMA describes a magic process: The function must be fulfilled without any equipment or apparatus (or with a minimum, like in Fantastic Analogy). This connection is rarely seen, but it is available, and I teach students to see it.

I also like to ascribe *unusual* magic features to objects. So as an improvement of the method, I make it even more difficult: I ask students to think of a TV that can magically transport the viewer to the place of action, i.e., to ascribe the function of transportation to something which has no wheels, etc. Swapping functions is sometimes even more original than the "natural" magic function like: tablecloth—eating; boots—jumping seven miles; or carpet—flying.

Checklist

Checklists are lists of questions, and the most famous checklists in creativity belong to Alex F. Osborn and Henry Poincaré (a French mathematician). For example, if you need to improve an object or to invent a new one, and questions in the checklist ask you to cut your object into pieces; to magnetize it; and to change the temperature to freezing, a checklist can definitely give you some hints.

Imagine that your task is to invent a new presentation method. A checklist would ask you: "Can you cut your presentation?" Probably yes, so what? No aha? The next question you read is: "Can you magnetize it?" And you think, "Hmm? It would be nice to have magnetically held posters on the board—something sticking to the board or wall . . . like a light dress sometimes sticks to the legs . . . Wow! Why not make the paper itself electrically charged for it to stick to any surface? Aha!!!"

Improvement: In my understanding, checklists are a version of the random word method, which works with lists of random words. However, they are preselected to give you the most diversified clues. So if we have climbed from a word list to a statement list, why not go further and introduce text lists? Text lists could give the person a pack of text with gaps to fill while thinking about the object under consideration.

Book Title ("Title")

William J.J. Gordon, who offered this technique, asked participants of the session to make up book titles consisting of two words opposed to each other and describing the object under consideration. For example, if you are asked to give a strange (and attractive) book title for such usual objects as a pen, pencil, stockings, etc., these book titles could look like: Short Longness (pen), Dirty Cleanness (pencil), Influential Weakness (stockings), etc. George Prince, the retired Chairman of Synectics, Inc., and Gordon's fellow pioneer, gives the following examples: Focused Desire (target), Balanced Confusion (mixture), Impure Aggressor (acid), Connected Pauses (machine gun bursts), etc. (For more information see Sidney J. Parnes' *Source Book for Creative Problem-Solving*, 1992.)

Improvement: As I mentioned above, Book Title and the whole variety of methods in Symbolic Analogy make a powerful trend of changing the object under consideration by working with symbols (names, signs, etc.), not the object itself. Variations are numerous: three word Book Title, five word Book Title, etc.

Semiotic Modeling ("SemiMod")

Created by Charles Pierce and Charles Morris, Semiotics is the science of signs. Semiotic Modeling is a generic name that I use for any type of sign/realm changing. You can go from text to visual props, or from one style of visual props to another style, or from one style of text to another style. For instance, if students make pictures (posters) while working on the text, this is Semiotic Modeling because they model some essence in the other semiotic means. If students rearrange scientific text into a poetic version or write a song about grammatical rules— they definitely change the realm of signs to another, or remodel the reflection. So fairy tales, pictures, or any other arts about science or vice versa all constitute types of Semiotic Modeling.

Semiotic Modeling is extremely useful from a strategic point of view: It helps to involve both right and left hemispheres in the work. In tactical applications, it forces students to see the object in a different way and, thus, causes fast changes in their point of view.

Famous examples of this method are: Quick Sketching, Mind-Mapping (for more information see the excellent books of Tony Buzan, including *The Mind Map Book*, 1993), Lesson Schemes, and any type of spatial learning.

Even making tables to organize data is a type of Semiotic Modeling. Morpho, by the way, belongs to this realm, too.

Dynamization ("Dyna")

Dynamization is the process of mentally changing one measurable parameter out of many to see what will happen with the essence. For example, any object has numerous measurable parameters like length, width, height, weight, color, temperature, etc. Dynamization, as a method, requires the change of only one parameter while keeping the others as they are.

Take, for instance, a comb. It has certain physical characteristics like length, etc. It also has certain number of teeth—let's say there are twenty of them. Now, imagine changing only this number without changing the material, weight, etc. If you go down to fifteen, it will be a comb for thick hair. If you go down to five, you have a rake. Go to three, and you have a trident. Go to two, and you have a hayfork. Go to one, and you have a back-scratcher or a toothpick. Now, go up from twenty to twenty-five, and (with the same thickness of the teeth) you have a comb for very thin hair. With thirty to forty, there might be no space for the hair—it becomes a waved ruler for an artist.

That is the way to see how quantitative parameters change the quality of the object. The leaps from one object to another are very obvious, and they connect objects into a strange chain.

Dynamization is extremely useful for checking the limits of the problem and for training your ability to see opposites. This method can produce a number of ideas to improve the vision of the original object.

Improvement: In our classes this method works for essence finding—you remember that a genius has the ability to see through to the essential. The moment we need to find an essence, we go to Dynamization. Variations are possible with changing two or more parameters, as well as changing other rules.

Vitalization ("Vita")

Vitalization is a method of ascribing live matter characteristics to a non-alive object, thus, totally changing the image of the object. For instance, live beings breathe, eat, move, dispose of waste, reproduce, etc. So having an object like a newspaper to improve, you ask, "How does the newspaper breathe? How does the newspaper eat? What does it eat? How does it reproduce itself? Changing a pretty familiar object like newspaper produces new original images and shapes.

Vitalization is a powerful method of changing the vision of one object and helping to see its hidden potentials.

Improvement: I explain Vitalization as a scientic version of personification and Personal Analogy in creative problem solving. Moreover, I make students theoretically explain the power of all three and the difference between all. It makes students see them as one method rather than three separate entities.

USING THE METHODS

In the mid 1980s, there were approximately 150 methods and techniques for creative problem solving. Today I am sure there are more than 200. You can find many of them in literature on creativity. There are modifications and there are new ones.

Now, how do you use these methods?

Imagine that you are in marketing, and your company is selling food made of chicken (chicken nuggets, chicken tenders, buffalo wings, etc.). You need a nice new advertising idea. To ignite your own imagination you take, for example, the method of Personal Analogy. You remember that you have to write a story starting with "I am a . . . " You choose an object—let's say the competitor's product (beef, cows), and you say, "I am a cow. I love my grass and green pastures. I like it when people take my milk. It tickles. The only thing I do not like is that they may slaughter me to eat. Hey people! Could you eat something else, like pigs or chicken? We cows would be very happy . . . " Aha! Here it comes! A famous phrase on a big billboard with three-dimensional cows: "Five out of five cows agree: 'Eat more chick'n!' "

When you face a problem and you're not certain what to do, think of all the methods you have at hand. Choose the method that is most appropriate. These are the methods used by geniuses. Also, remember: If they do not fit your problem, feel free to improve! This will certainly help you on your path to genius. Soon your creative ability will develop into a bright flame leading others through darkness. The ideas you generate and innovations you introduce will have endurance without death.

Chapter Fourteen

Determine Your Next Move

If there is faith that can move mountains, it is faith
in your own power.

MARIE VON EBNER-ESCHENBACH

Before we start this chapter, I want you to recall that there
are five levels of nature development, five levels of human
society development, five levels of knowledge development, five levels of education, and so on. I am sure you
will not be surprised to know that there are five different
types of geniuses and five steps to becoming a genius.

The exercises in the previous chapters were directed at
developing, maintaining, and insuring the core genius features in your character. They were not easy to do, but they
led you to the transformation from genius features into ge-
nius activities—genius visioning (step one), genius communicating (step two), genius thinking (step three), genius orientation (step four), and genius acting (step five).

Well, you are becoming a genius! The question is: What
type of a genius are you becoming or, perhaps more to the
point, where and how do you want to apply your genius?
Let's examine each of the general types of geniuses and

determine your next steps in putting your genius into action.

- Existential genius
- Communicational genius
- Instrumental genius
- Orientational genius
- Innovational genius

All of these types are needed, but they are perceived and recognized differently. They represent the whole field of geniuses. You may aim at any type in your activities.

EXISTENTIAL GENIUS

Existential genius is the genius of survival. This type is capable of surviving under any circumstances—deserted island, desert, jungle, no money, no place to live. The art of survival is extremely important. Our ancestors had to have the genius to survive, or we would not be here now. With billions deceased, billions destroyed, and billions neglected and left to die, we are the descendents of survivors—those who were more creative and more talented, and who were geniuses in the art of survival. We owe them our gratitude and respect.

Let's consider the following example of existential genius. During the Vietnam war, an American officer, Lt. Col. Iceal Hambleton, was recovered from enemy territory in northern South Vietnam after eleven and a half days on the ground in an area that contained thirty thousand enemy troops. Maybe you remember the movie *Bat-21* that portrayed the rescue of Lt. Col. Hambleton on screen. Intense ground fire prevented the first rescue attempts. Then a plan was devised to direct him by radio contact to a safer pickup point. The rescue team knew that Hambleton, an avid golfer, remembered in great detail various golf courses where he had played. So, to guide him safely past enemy camps, units, and unfriendly villages to a rescue point, specific holes at certain courses were used to establish distance and direction of travel for each segment of his journey. This was done so that the enemy, listening on radio, could not follow the directions and capture Hambleton, as he had a great deal of valuable intelligence information. (See details at the U.S. Air Force Rescue Service Web page at www.wpafb.af.mil/museum/history/res cue/res13a.htm.) The plan for using golf courses was a stroke (excuse the pun) of creative genius.

Such an air crash could happen in a jungle, a desert, or in any other place of great natural barriers. Dr. E. Paul Torrance was first called to teach creativity to the U.S. Air Force—and it was a survival creativity course, not engineering, not communication, not commanding troops—just survival. It is interesting to see how real historical events corroborate our theory: the existential level first! Even the creativity theory is applied first to the level of existence of survival. Now they teach courses in existential (survival) creativity in all the armed forces.

A lot of creativity is needed to survive. Often resources are limited. Earlier I cited Abraham Maslow, the founder of the self-actualization theory of creativity, who said that a first-rate soup is more creative than a second-rate painting. What he actually stated is that there is creativity of the existential level—the level where soup is important, the level where we need to be creative just to survive.

A single parent has to be creative. A parent of a large

family who makes food from limited resources has to be creative. It is not what people traditionally call creativity, but it is creativity—it is finding new solutions for everyday existential problems.

My friend Dr. Kobus Neethling, the founder of South African Creativity Foundation and the author of numerous best-sellers, gave a speech at the Dr. E. Paul Torrance Annual Lecture series at the University of Georgia. He mentioned that millions of South Africans need everyday creativity to determine how to bring water from a well located four miles away. (For more information, see *The Future of Creativity* published by Scholastic Testing Services in 2002.) He did not call it existential creativity, but it is this creativity and this existential genius that he was talking about.

In the Jewish culture, the story of survival is extremely important. Jews have survived all the oppressors, all the conquests, all the migrations, all the language and political changes, and even the Holocaust. These myriad survivals required existential genius, and this existential genius is mentioned in every service, and is recognized and honored.

From Creativity to MegaCreativity in Existence

If existential creativity fits your needs or desires, perhaps you want to focus on it, as opposed to the other types. Perhaps you would like to be a MegaCreator in this field. You can do it! Now that you know the principles of Mega-Creativity, it is at your service.

You know how to build the matrix, you know how to fill it with various creative ideas, and you know how to take your time by combining ideas. It will be MegaCreativity on the existential level, or existential MegaCreativity.

environment		
house		
door		
wall		
window		
room		
ceiling		
street		
vocabulary (words)		
yard		

Living, eating, walking, sleeping, breathing, and all other functions of the biological (physiological) level are involved in this level of existence. Remember this, and feel free to be creative.

Millions of people before you spent years trying to make this level easier. They wanted us to progress, and so they invented, built, and improved. They did this to liberate us from the need to spend most of our time on the existential level. However, let's not forget about the need for existential creativity. Let's train our children in the basics. Someday, when necessity strikes, they will thank their teachers—you and me. Two of my school graduates, Charlie and Tim Wilkins, have achieved high ranks in the Boy Scouts, which gives them many skills on the existential level. Their goals lay in other types of genius (one will be an athlete and the other will be an artist), but they have learned how to survive, and if life brings troubles, I am sure they will continue to survive.

What Is Your Next Move?

So think of your next move. Please remember, 90 percent of success lies in being present, in existing. Your task at this level, therefore, is to continue to exist, to come to the next stage, to be present at the next event, to be in a better position for continuing your work. If you would like to be MegaCreative at this level, ask yourself this question: How can you change your existence in such a way that there are millions of other positive consequences?

For example, in 1992 I was invited to be the first Russian student at the U.S. Air Force Air War College. As a Russian colonel, I planned to go back to my country after completing the training. My Doctor of Science dissertation was waiting for me there, written, polished, and ready for defending. However, upon graduating in 1993, my family and I decided to stay in the United States where we could practice our newly found religious freedom. At the time, there was only one synagogue in Moscow—and even that one was constantly under attack.

The transition to a new country and a new way of life required MegaCreativity on an existential level. My wife and I were the first Russian couple in Montgomery, Alabama, and had to adapt to a new culture, a new climate, and a new way of living. I remember this time, and I especially recall one moment—the moment of existential discovery. During the first six months, we visited many churches and talked to many different congregations. It was a great experience—there was so much variety in the services and in the people. While we were attending a service at Temple Beth Or, my wife suddenly burst into tears. As she could barely explain through her weeping, the Rabbi (Dr. David Baylinson) was saying the same words her father used to tell her as a young girl in Russia, but now she was hearing them in English. It was a revelation to her. As people seated around us learned why she had begun to cry, they too were moved. They embraced her. They accepted her. They calmed her down. After this day, there were hundreds of "Aha!" moments rippling through our lives as well as through the life of the temple. My wife was rediscovering her Jewish heritage in the customs and traditions that her family preserved without calling them Jewish (being a Jew is pretty dangerous in Russia). Now, suddenly, all her past and all her present were connected with the light of understanding. That was a revelation, and its power is still touching the lives of everyone who was in the temple that day, especially when we became American citizens.

This change in my life—going from a Russian military colonel to an American—was obviously an existential change that led to millions of other changes: my way of living, my way of relating to people, the tools used, the problems needing to be solved and, finally, the innovations to be introduced. The whole spectrum of five levels was altered because of one change. Many people since then have told me that one has to have guts for that. I just agree.

In the same manner, a person can choose a university

to study at, a profession to learn, a company to work with, a place to live—one change that will lead to millions of everyday changes.

Be wise in your choices. Beware of the consequences. Remember, your new capabilities and the moment you use them may be the moment of change that will modify your whole life.

So, what is your next move? A move so deep, so basic, so existentially founded that it will bring not one but millions of changes? Write it down.

COMMUNICATIONAL GENIUS

Communicational genius is, of course, the genius of communication—the ability to communicate one's way through any circumstances, troubles, or problems. The art of communicating is extremely important. For over five million years, verbal communication has been developing as the next step above nonverbal communication, which is as old as living matter. Verbal communication is much more powerful and progressive and has accelerated the development of all humankind.

Our communication, whether we understand it fully or not, is the highest art and the highest skill developed by nature. Our ancestors had to be able to express themselves, their goals, and their opinions. Most importantly, they had to communicate in order to create communities and to work with others. Those who communicated better created better teams, survived many difficulties, and solved the next level of problems. Whether through a prayer, a joke, or a plan, those who communicated creatively were better able to survive and succeed. The best ones would become communicational geniuses.

History has many examples of communicational geniuses. They are not famous for their survival skills, like conquerors of the North Pole. They are not famous for their inventions, like Thomas Edison, or for their discoveries, like Michael Faraday or Marie Curie. Communicational geniuses are famous for their outstanding communication that created something outstanding for society.

For example, we find communicational genius in the *Thousand and One Arabian Nights*. For several years a cruel and distrustful king (once cheated on by his wife) had been marrying a new virgin every day and killing this woman the next morning. The country was running out of young women, and finally Sheherazade, the eldest daughter of the grand wizard, found a way to tame the king. She bravely stepped onto the path that led so many to death. She prevented her own execution by telling half of a very interesting story and promising to tell the second half the next day. The next day, however, she told the end of the story and started a new one. She managed to do it for 1,001 nights until the old king died.

Look at this famous story from an analytical point of view. Sheherazade had to be a communicational genius to survive. Her genius was not in hiding, not in running away, and not in fleeing from the country; she found a communicational solution for an existential problem. She survived, her sister (who listened with the king and who wrote all the stories every evening) survived, and her father, the grand wizard, also survived. By this act, she also managed to save hundreds of young women. A genius solution!

In ancient Greece, communication skills (rhetoric) were highly developed and respected. Rhetoric was taught first together with fighting, and then (excuse my pun) as the art of fighting without fighting. Public speaking became a power in itself. Later, it became a separate subject at many schools around the world. Only recently was it pushed out of the curriculum by silent and simplified multiple-choice tests. What a loss!

Communicational genius, as you see, is finding communicational solutions for communicational and even noncommunicational problems. Instead of fighting for freedom—going to the barricades and shooting—a communicational genius tells stories about a tyrant and creates sharp nicknames, anecdotes, humor, mocking jokes, and communicational traps—all the communicational solutions. Laughter, as you know, is the most dangerous weapon of all—at least for tyrants.

We have benefited from a number of communicational geniuses in our times, such as Martin Luther King Jr., who inspired the entire country to recognize and stop the unfair treatment of African Americans. Others in the Civil Rights movement used violent methods, but King used the power of his words, which had a much greater effect than sticks or guns. Although he was killed decades ago, his words remain inspirational—a communicational solution to an existential problem.

MegaCreativity in Communication

To reach the peak of communicational genius, try to find ways to progress more quickly from whatever stage you find yourself in now. List all the parameters of nonverbal and verbal communication, and aim for perfection in all of them to make yourself a communicational genius (an outstanding communicator). Develop this list into a powerful matrix with all the variety of speeches, presentations, and communicational situations.

environment		
nonverbal		
pose		
mimics		
distance		
voice pitch		
voice volume		
speed of speech		
accents		
vocabulary (words)		
grammar		
style		

You know how to build the matrix, you know how to fill it with various creative ideas, and you know how to take your time by combining ideas. It will be your Mega-

Creativity on the communicational level, or communicational MegaCreativity.

What Is Your Next Move?

Now that you understand the nature of communicational genius, are you interested in making this field your focus? Are you at ease with friends and strangers? Do people listen to you automatically?

Sometimes a student needs to change just one feature to make great strides in this field. For example, I worked with a teacher who had a habit of blocking herself and looking down. We changed that in the first four hours, and her whole life changed. In another case, I had a person in a seminar who had never been promoted. It took only six minutes to change his handshake, and he was promoted within three months. Look at how one feature can change you. Or, you may need to develop a whole different way of communicating with higher trust, reliability, support, intimacy, love, and creativity.

Imagine that your communication is like a river: If it is narrow, it is fast and rough; if it is broad, it is soothing and calming. Maybe it is time to think how you can make your river basin broader, how you can remove some obstacles from your powerful flow of impeccable communication.

So, what is your next move? A move so deep, so basic, so profound that it will bring not one or two but millions of changes to your communicational life and other levels of your life, too? Write it down and make a plan to achieve it! Think how you can make your communication so differ-

ent and innovative that you will make a huge difference
and will be remembered as a genius.

_____

_____

_____

_____

_____

INSTRUMENTAL GENIUS

I have to confess that at first I wanted to put Socrates
among the communicational geniuses. He was often like
a gadfly—he was sharp and sarcastic, and his solutions
were seemingly communicational. Later, however, my
analysis showed that he wasn't. His wife beat him many
times right in the middle of the market for his intimidating
way of communicating. He also failed to defend himself
in court where he was charged with spoiling the youth of
Greece. As a result of this failure, he was given a choice:
either leave the great city of Athens, or die. He preferred
to drink a cup of hemlock—the poison used at that time.
At court, he failed to change his speech style from the
sharp sarcasm he used at the market into legal speech. He
embarrassed the judges, and sadly, paid for it in the end.

Socrates failed as a communicational genius but was
actually a different type of genius. He created *moral
philosophy*—an instrument that would be used by millions
of people after his death. Another famous instrument he
introduced was the so-called Socratic dialogue—the

method of teaching by which a teacher asks questions and thus leads students to the answers rather than just lecturing or instructing. How many young minds became active thanks to this method? Millions.

Instrumental genius is the creation of new instruments and tools, new methods and techniques. Figuratively speaking, instrumental geniuses are those who make the buttons that other people will press.

The best of the instrumental geniuses are called *golden hands* and sometimes *golden heads*. It means the person's hands or head is as valuable as gold; they find the best (fastest, most reliable, most efficient) solutions. An instrumental genius is the person who thinks about others, who tries to make their lives easier by creating tools and instruments, methods and techniques to help. These tools and methods are the continuation of the person's genius. They may save millions of hours of somebody's labor. They may save billions of dollars because a new tool makes the job easier and faster. They may save millions of lives, like in the case of new surgical tools.

Instrumental innovations are different from communicational innovations. They look artificial, and they *are* artificial. Nature doesn't create instruments; they are only made by humans.

Thinking about new instruments, making new instruments, and using new instruments is so fundamentally powerful that this is certainly a field of human genius. A new instrument can range from a new theory to a new brick—like the one invented by Alden B. Dow, a famous architect, a theorist, and a practitioner of creativity. [For more information, see *Creating Creativity: 101 Defini-*

tions (What Webster Never Told You) published by Alden B. Dow Creativity Center Press in 2000].

Another example of a brilliant instrument is the invention of Esperanto. Esperanto is an artificial, or "planned," language created by L.L. Zamenhof in Poland. This language is so simple that it can be learned in weeks—a tremendous acceleration from the time required to learn a foreign language! At present there are over 300,000 people who speak Esperanto all over the world and over 4000 books translated into Esperanto. Thus, you can enjoy Shakespeare in a strange looking but very simple form. (All genius solutions are simple!)

Science is an instrument of instruments. It makes them necessary and predetermines the creation of new instruments. From studying creativity, I felt there was a need for a science focused on newness, so I created a new science: Novology. This is an instrument for seeing things that were earlier unseen.

When science is recognized as an instrument to help us better understand nature and as an instrument for accelerating natural results, it becomes an unstoppable force. Also, stepping into the realm of scientific research moves a person to a field where the genius level is more possible to achieve.

The introduction of Novology as a new science and a new vision of the world brought numerous innovative results. Certainly, if newness is discovered and understood as an objectively existing phenomenon, it must be measured, calculated, compressed into regularities, generalized into laws, and studied by a separate new science. Novology did it. It introduced ways to define and measure newness. It introduced special units for measuring newness. It formulated regularities and laws. It built the foundation for other research activities.

This change in the theoretical foundations has brought numerous practical results. They have been implemented by numerous successful educational programs, from the Russian Academy of Sciences to Fortune 500 companies, as well as elite universities and remote colleges and schools. The programs have helped thousands of people become more creative and innovative and, therefore, more productive and useful members of society.

Instrumental MegaCreativity

So perhaps you want to be an instrumental genius, creating a new science. Go for it. If your interests and talents lay in medicine or art or technology, focus your attention in those fields. Create a table and begin using your Mega-Creativity. To achieve the genius level, think in broad terms and push yourself beyond creating a single instrument. Think in terms of trends. For example, if you focus on art, push beyond creating a single painting or sculpture. Try to create a new vision of painting, such as Picasso did when he invented Cubism.

If your interests are in the field of business, use the matrix to create a new business instrument. Traditionally, innovation in business is roughly divided into administrative and technical innovations. Instrumental innovation as described in this book is closer to traditionally understood technical innovation. Instrumental innovation is either paid for (by buying new instruments) or is produced by internal effort (research and development). In both cases, it may be expensive. However, without instrumental innovation, there is no way to beat competitors and stay on the cutting edge. Companies that fail to seek instrumental innovations are doomed.

Okay, you know how to use the matrix. Begin.

What Is Your Next Step?

New tools and new instruments make true geniuses produce new tools. These new tools allow humanity to quickly achieve new levels; therefore, a happy humanity honors the inventors as geniuses.

Well, consider a tool to make.

Could you give it a shot and invent one of the following?

- a new material instrument
- a new ideal instrument
- a new methodology—a new way to use instruments to achieve higher or faster results

Think of how you could innovate on the instrumental level, that is, in the field of producing new tools. You know now who makes the buttons (tools, instruments, methods, techniques). You can make the buttons, too! Try it, use it, and become an instrumental genius. What will you do?

_____

_____

_____

_____

_____

_____

ORIENTATIONAL GENIUS

No instrument, never mind how powerful, is helpful until it is oriented to the needs of society. Orientational genius is the level where all the existential skills, all the communicational skills, and all the instrumental skills come together to be oriented for the solution of a social problem or problems. The larger the problem, the higher the probability of becoming a genius. It's that simple. This is also the level where innovative minds and actions dramatically accelerate problem solving itself.

Examples of orientational geniuses are numerous. The United States as a whole is an orientational genius. Russians teach children at school that Pavel N. Yablochkov invented the first electric light; even if this is true, Thomas Edison made it a system of electrical bubbles and wires and nets that were needed for it to work (orientation is different). Russians teach children at school that Alexander Popov invented the radio (Radio Day is celebrated in Russia); but even if this is true, Guglielmo Marconi made the device we know and use as a radio (different orientation). U.S. Air Force officers told me that a Russian mathematician created the theory of the stealth plane, but Americans built it (different orientation). Look at Neuro Linguistics: Alexander R. Luria published a book about it, but Americans made Neuro Linguistic Programming (NLP), a system for using Neuro Linguistics for convincing people, which created more effective sales techniques and educational techniques.

There are hundreds of cases like that—not only with Russians, but also with other nations. Americans are pragmatically implementing all the best new ideas available in the world. Americans borrow words. Americans borrow concepts, theories, and models. Americans orient the newness found in the world to solve everyday practical problems for the betterment of all societies.

Americans are certainly producing new ideas, new products, and new services by themselves, too. However, they are also open to ideas from around the world. More-over, Americans, who need more and more new ideas, create numerous methods for producing new ideas. Brainstorming was just the first of them.

Speaking of Americans, I truly believe that the creators of the free-market system were geniuses of the orientational level. They did not invent every element of it, but they combined all the known elements to make the creation successful. The founders of American society created the Constitution and a political system that doesn't contradict the free-market system. Thus, they allowed the creative juices of their people to develop the existential, communicational, instrumental, orientational, and innovational aspects of American society. No wonder now the United States is the world's leader in innovation. Looking back, the founders of America intuitively found the elixir of successful social life; believe it or not, the basic ingredient of this elixir was newness and allowing this newness to flow.

With cities named New York, New London, and New Orleans, and states named New Mexico and New Hampshire, America's newness was attractive to many people. The country of newness celebrated its newness. If analyzed from this point of view, American society introduced and accepted:

- New World (*freedom of existence*: live separately from Europe, away from old orders, old kings, old religions; also, *freedom of movement*).
- Freedom of speech (*freedom of communication*).
- Free-market economy (*freedom of choosing instruments*—what to do and how to do it).

- Democracy (*freedom of choosing social orientation*—people to help, sell, do business with, build parties, coalitions, associations, and so on).
- Openness (*freedom of innovating*—where and how to produce and consume newness).

As you can see, there are the same five levels found by Novology, but they are not structured scientifically. The italicized words represent our system, the Novology system of levels. It is amazing that without any science they created a social entity that is self-sustaining and developing faster than other societies. Glory to those who intuitively find the right path!

The Soviet system, the USSR, on the contrary, when analyzed from the same point of view, was opposed to newness from all sides:

- No freedom of movement (passport registration, closed cities, closed regions).
- No freedom of speech (you could be easily sent to jail or to a mental hospital for a "political" joke).
- No freedom of tools (they must be Marxist and Leninist tools).
- No freedom of business (all business is government controlled).
- No freedom of innovation (censorship, no copy machines, no patents—all ideas belong to the government, closed borders, Berlin Wall and Iron Curtain).

The result of the suppression of newness and innovation is well known. From the point of view of Novology, no wonder the Soviet Union and the Soviet system lost in the economic, social, political, and military competition. They actually failed to follow the fundamental laws of nature: the laws of Novology.

We can firmly state it now: It is the accepting of newness or the oppressing of newness that makes social formations live or die. This rule applies also to businesses and people. By the way, even though Novology was conceived in Russia, the article and the book on Novology were published in the United States. For me, it's symbolic that Novology, the science of newness, is celebrated in the land of newness.

Novology as a science is still a science. It must be oriented to solving societal problems to be helpful; it must be applied. The number of applications is growing. In addition to Creative Problem Solving, Novology offers Innovative Problem Solving (IPS). The latter makes people the center of the solution. It makes them tolerant, willing to change, active in changing, and ready to work hard for change and innovation. Innovative Problem Solving offers an absolutely different approach—change people, help people change, solve first the people part of the innovation puzzle, and then make the change. MegaValue people; all the rest is solvable. Firing people, laying off employees, or in simple words "throwing them away" will create numerous other problems. Innovative solutions find the opportunities rather than seek problems. Innovative leaders will solve the problems automatically by finding a proper opportunity and embarking on it.

This innovative approach is open to the future. It focuses on the future rather than on the present, and it focuses on people rather than on processes and objects.

That is why the innovative approach brings forward new methodologies for education.

What Is Your Next Move?

The orientational level is extremely difficult to achieve. To be successful, people on this level must have all the features of the previous levels. They have to *survive* the troubles of growth. They have to become outstanding *communicators*. They have to become masters of the *instrumental* level. In addition, they have to be able to *orient* their knowledge and creativity to modern and future world problems.

Give it a shot. Try to find a world problem and solve it. Think of how you could innovate on the orientational level in the field of solving people's problems. Can you find an idea or a solution that would solve an existing problem faster?

What is your next problem to solve? What problems require your attention? What problems are troubling humanity? What problems are you ready to dedicate your life to? What problems will keep you awake at night?

Be honest. Be frank. Are you concerned with people's problems? Would you like to help them? Remember that there are no geniuses who solved problems for themselves—otherwise, robbing a bank might be a genius action. Sorry, but those who have not developed a social consciousness and who are not ready to work for others are not candidates for the genius title.

So find a worthy purpose, write it here, and try to use all the methods we've discussed or those you've created on your own to solve a social problem.

_____

_____

_____

_____

_____

_____

_____

What will you be thinking about?
- Smart (original, genuine, new) solutions to increase the speed of processes in every field.
- Faster training and education works in every field.
- Higher inventiveness in all areas.

Be a creative problem solver—the fastest possible. Become an orientational genius: Find a difficult problem facing the world today, and apply all known methods to it. See the roots of the problem, not the superficial level. Find the cause, or the uni-cause, and then find the treatment for this cause. If the problem cannot be solved with known methods, invent new methods. There are no problems that cannot be solved. Find the biggest, the most fundamental. You can move mountains, as the epigraph of this chapter says. You have to have faith in your own power.

Chapter Fifteen

Accelerate Your Innovational Genius

What we need are more people who specialize in the impossible.

THEODORE ROETHKE

In this chapter we'll discuss the highest level of genius: innovational genius. We explored the innovational approach in the previous chapter, but now we'll focus on the highest form of innovation: innovation in the field of innovation. At this level, we combine aspects of all the other fields of genius. Our path to this level is achieved by following the five laws of MegaCreativity:

1. Quit Quitting
2. Why Not Every (K)not?
3. Go for a Million
4. Mega-Value People
5. Launch to the Genius Orbit

By now you have committed these laws to memory and have looked for ways to apply them in your life. Here's a story of how I applied them in my life and achieved the results I wanted. It was this episode that made me think differently and act differently in the field of innovation.

When I got my Ph.D., I was transferred to Moscow and became a professor of the Military Institute. I was happy to learn that the institute had its own publishing program and its own magazine. After a few months on the faculty, I brought an article to the magazine about a new model of education. Ten days later I was called to a meeting and was told that the magazine is an "academic publication and it does not publish geometry." Despite my attempts to explain that it was a Graph Theory (not geometry) and that it was just a graphic model (not a theorem), they turned down my article. Hmm . . . this was a new experience for me. A military bureaucrat with a bulldog face looked at me as if I were an intruder in the sacred garden of academic serenity. I didn't like that. The next day I took the article to the Russian Academy of Sciences (the highest level in the Soviet scientific hierarchy). They laughed at my story of the institute's rejection, read the article, accepted it for publication, asked if I had anything else to publish, and published four of my articles in the next two issues of their books. The next year, I received a call from my "own" military editor (same face), asking why I chose not to publish with my own institute's magazine.

As you can see from the example, my innovation was first slowed down (bureaucracy hates innovation), but if you are persistent and you know that there is value in what you're doing, go to the next level. Actually, this refusal was a benefit to me. The Russian Academy of Sciences became my second home, and many other developments came from this connection.

Perhaps you have had a similar experience. If your efforts and ideas were rejected, how did you respond? If you accepted the rejection and abandoned your idea, consider reviving it. This time use the laws of MegaCreativity. Here is how those steps applied to my situation with the institute's magazine.

- **Quit Quitting!** I went to the other publisher when I was rejected by my own institute.
- **Why Not Every (K)not!** I questioned the "no" answer.
- **Go for a Million!** I was published by the Russian Academy of Sciences, where millions of people could read my articles.
- **MegaValue People!** Now through the Academy of Sciences, I was teaching employers and employees to value people.
- **Launch to the Genius Level!** I was innovating— finding ways to introduce millions of new things into the educational and business areas.

Before moving to the next section, take a moment and remember a situation in which you could have applied the five laws of MegaCreativity. How could the outcome have been different for you? How could it have been more positive and a true expression of your genius? Next, think of a situation in which you're involved today—a problem you're facing in your job, perhaps, or a problem facing your company. Perhaps you are stuck while writing a novel or the class you are teaching is not responding the way you want. Perhaps you are a true citizen of the world and would like to solve worldwide problems, such as world hunger or the political strife in the Middle East. How could you apply the five laws to any of these problems and achieve the level of innovational genius?

INNOVATIONAL GENIUS

The level of innovational genius is the most difficult level to achieve. This is the level where innovative minds and actions dramatically accelerate innovation itself. Actually, this is the level of accelerating the acceleration.

A brilliant example of accelerating the process of innovation can be seen in Doug Hall and his creativity center, called the Eureka! Ranch.

Doug invites twenty to thirty employees from a company, including leaders, to his center. Then he complements the client's team with a team of his own trained people. He arranges a day of bombarding their brains with various stimuli and, as a response, gets about two thousand ideas. His group works through the night, sifting through the ideas and combining them into two hundred perspective groups. The next day Doug works only with the leadership group to create twelve to twenty ideas polished to the peak level: They are not only ideas—they are packed ideas (pictures, boxes, menus, whatever is invented). As a result, after forty-eight hours of hyperintensive labor, the company leaders get twelve to twenty ready-to-go product visions.

Hall is accelerating the process of innovation from around five years to forty-eight hours, or about nine hundred times (364 days a year $\times$ 5 years = 1820 days : 2 days = 910!). Imagine how much labor is saved, how many salaries are not wasted, and how many minds are free to work on other problems! Doug also makes it fun. He saves companies millions of dollars, and he sends them to the competitive edge in no time. Finally, he states that the process is scientifically sound, and he claims that it's at least six times more powerful than brainstorming.

Doug has found a way to accelerate the acceleration. He uses all his natural and learned creativity to accelerate the process of innovation. These accomplishments and his ability to communicate these methods to others place him at the level of innovational genius.

INNOVATIONAL GENIUS IN PUBLISHING

In my experience, there is a case of accelerating innovation even to a higher speed. It happened in October 2001 at the Seventh International Creativity Conference in Klein Kariba (near Pretoria), South Africa. Over two hundred conference participants—business and education leaders of South Africa and international presenters—attempted to establish two world records:
- the fastest written book
- the fastest published book

The book, titled *Making the Impossible Possible: 200 Plus Creative Ideas*, was written in four minutes and thirty seconds. It was published in fifteen hours and fifty-eight minutes. Imagine the excitement among the participants when they received the book the next day! The book became a symbol of making the impossible possible. We hope to one day see it listed in the *Guinness Book of World Records*. Moreover, according to our agreement, all the proceeds from the sale of the book will go to the Nelson

Mandela Children's Fund. Thus we will help South African children.

I have to tell you that this project was not an overnight event. The history of this attempt included the following steps:

1. It took us fourteen months: four months for gathering definitions and ten months for publishing the book *Creating Creativity: 101 Definitions (What Webster Never Told You)*.

2. In May 2000 at the American Creativity Association Annual Convention in Chicago, Illinois, I was the featured keynote speaker (or as they called it, the Featured Creativity Igniter) with the topic "MegaCreativity: New Speeds for the New Millennium," I attempted to write a book in less than ten minutes—during the keynote speech. As a result of this effort, the book, preliminary titled, *Wow! MegaCreativity*, was written by fifty-eight participants in eight minutes and forty-three seconds. The progress of compressing the writing process was vivid: We leaped from four months to several minutes. However, the book is still in the publishing stage. The creativity process was accelerated, but the innovation process was not.

3. In July 2000 at the Eleventh International Conference on Creativity in Universities and Colleges at Northwood University in Midland, Michigan, I teamed up with Lisa Spragens, an innovation specialist from Procter and Gamble, to develop a new innovation process. As a result of our effort, the book *Loving Creativity* was written by fifty-seven participants in five minutes and was published within thirty-six hours. The faces and the eyes of those

who were published for the first time told me that it was worth doing. What a pleasure!

Let me state it here: The participants' reaction was so highly positive because it seemed impossible. This highly positive reaction triggered several other cases of accelerated publishing made by MegaInnovative Mind International Institute. In all of them, the participants were so proud to get their works published that it naturally led our team to the idea of using this for our educational work. This is how the project called Author's Pride came into being.

Franklin Junior High School in Franklin, Ohio, embarked on the project at once. Principal John Magee, a retired US Navy captain, was faster than the others. A month later, on November 16–18, 2002, the book titled *And the World Would Be a Better Place* was written in four minutes and forty-five seconds and was published in forty-eight hours. The local newspaper editorial called the students "Instant Authors."

You should've seen the faces of these kids when the book was handed to them. This was a moment of excitement, happiness, and enormous enthusiasm! This was a moment of author's pride which we hope will lead children to being poets, writers, reporters, scientists, scholars, etc., instead of turning to drugs, violence, and other trouble. Franklin Junior High School also became the first school in the world where all the students are published authors!

The project was a success! The overall meaning of the project was clear. In addition to this, from the scientific point of view, it was most important that the writing process was accelerated 25,000 times (from four months to five minutes) and that the publishing process was accelerated about 150 times (from ten months to forty-eight hours). As you can see, it's not just doubling (200 percent) or even tripling (300 percent) the speed—it's increasing the speed of production hundreds or thousands of times. We can easily call that an accelerated innovation breakthrough.

What Is Your Next Move?

From the previous two cases, you can see how innovation can be applied to the field of innovation. What is your field of endeavor? Think about the ways innovation takes place in your field, and find ways to accelerate it. This will be your innovation in the field of innovation. Become an innovational genius! Know what you are doing and do it. If the speed of your innovation is higher than the speed of your competitors, then you are the winner. Speed! Speed! Speed!

As we have done with the other genius fields, let's make a table and begin. You know the process well by now. It's your turn to try it on your own. Make your table and begin. Or perhaps by now you have applied your MegaCreative mind even to this process and you have invented a new one. If so, use it.

What does it take to become a famous school, a famous conference, or a famous company? Courage and decisiveness! A courageous principal makes the difference. A courageous director, president, or CEO makes the difference. True leaders are always ahead. True leaders are always looking for the most powerful instruments to get to the cutting edge and to stay there. True leaders are innovating with the highest speed, and they are also innovating in the field of innovation. Be a leader!

Epilogue

> To believe in something not yet proved and to
> underwrite it with our lives; it is the only way we can
> leave the future open.
>
> LILLIAN SMITH

We live on Earth, and we dream, build, and aspire to more. Where will our dreams take us? Will the next generation of innovators live in underwater paradises, or will they watch the Earth rise over the moon's horizon from a space base? Will we travel into our solar system or beyond? Humans are a species that cannot be limited. Everything is possible. As Jennifer Page, a graduate of the School of Geniuses, once said, "There are no limitations outside those you set for yourself and choose to live within." We have explored a world about which we once knew nothing. We have cured diseases once thought incurable, and we have tamed many natural forces.

There is an airport in Japan on a huge man-made island. There is a base in orbit where people live. It is the challenge of creators and innovators—the task of geniuses—not only to figure out the next step, but also all the steps beyond. Avoid limiting yourself, your mind, or your dreams, and you will have already won the toughest battle anyone can fight. Apply the five laws of MegaCreativity to any problem or any situation, and you will discover the solution.

Quit Quitting

Why Not Every (K)not?

Go for a Million

MegaValue People

Launch to the Genius Orbit

It may sound paradoxical, but all that you see around you—the material world—will pass away. The only real thing we have is our dreams that will become the new reality; they will live in our future deeds and future creations, and those who will reach for them will live forever.

Full speed ahead, my genius friends. You are the future geniuses of the Earth.

Index